Cover: 'Eseis', Alberto Ballocca

FIDALMA LOTTI

PREFERABLY THE ORIGINAL, RATHER THAN THE DIGITAL

THE ULTIMATE DIY ART GENERATOR

Preferably the original, rather than the digital

The world of traditional arts no longer exists, at least it is not the only alternative. Nowadays Non-Fungible Tokens represent a complementary market to traditional art systems, as well as the main source of scarcity for digital artworks.

This book collects some artworks selected from artists who have decided to collaborate on this project.

It all began when I made the decision to attend a small call for bids with other colleagues, proposing some of our digitally developed works.

In the announcement it was requested to send preferably the original project rather than the digital one, even if we mainly make digital works, (which however can be printed).

After asking for some clarification, we have been told that digital works would have been accepted, increasing the evaluation of our project if we would have put our hands on it - once printed – e.g. painting on it.

The main issue was not the rejection of digitally created works (anyone is free to use specific parameters to award a call for bids) but the matter of understanding the digitally developed works.

Asking an author to put hands on their digital work it means to consider it as "incomplete", needing something that makes it original.

What would the original work be? The one we designed or a paper copy revisited in an artisanal way?

The project consists in a paper catalogue representing some copies of artworks taken from Opensea as a colouring book, with the aim of criticizing the conception of art as a result of a single material (and textured) process.

In this colouring book the relationship between material and digital is set on two levels:

1) original artwork is the digital one through the NFT and its copy is the material page of the book

2) making the digital to correspond the "original": readers will finally be able to "make original" the authors' artworks by manipulating the printed copy.

The book is a catalogue showing reproductions of several NFTs - of which I am not the owner, so it would be a printed copy of a digital copy.

It is not conceived as a collection, but mainly as a single work, so people who do not understand digital art can have printed versions, bounded in a single and physical work.

For them, this may not be enough to make a work as the original one. Because of this all readers could be artists and finally make the original authors' works as the original ones, by scribbling, colouring, reassembling it and so on, following (or not following) the instruction on the opposite page.

The world of NFTs, even the micro world that includes this book, is constantly evolving and changing while I am writing these words. Some works have already been withdrawn from the market or transferred to other platforms, so in fact this book is already partially obsolete even before printing it.

One of the first lessons learned from the NFT world is that I would not have known a wide range of artists if they had not decided to put their works in NFT marketplaces, which have opened to them a global channel outside the traditional art market so far.

This aspect is also reflected in the network between artists; as in pre-NFT world artists are often collectors of artists who are their friends, appreciated as people or colleagues; probably some of the mentioned artists, viewing the book for the first time, will find works coming by artists they know, follow or maybe they have already collected.

The main platform used to select the works is Opensea where everything is, as the word itself, an open sea; apart from the trending collections, artworks can be filtered or ordered through some features related to their placing on the market; this type of filters obviously often have showed me generative artists, probably because they set in motion a greater number of transactions.

However, I wanted to include different types of artists in the project and, in order to optimize the research, I used the artists' network as a parameter to select the artworks. From a single artist's profile, it is also possible to see NFTs they have collected and the related authors; often artists repeated themselves over and over in their colleagues' collections but sometimes I received unexpected results.
In this sense, the support between

artists, including both artistic and financial matters, has been crucial even in a virtual world where your potential target seems almost unlimited.

Navigating in this open sea I discovered an artist who had uploaded a collection of his works that had been censored on other channels.
Freeing an artwork from a strict physical dimension and showing it to an interconnected and shared world could mitigate the risk of censorship.
Obviously, the digital world is not without risks due to conditions of use - Instagram continues to censor Canova's statues, not recognizing them as art - but there is also a tacit and subtle censorship given by the art market, according to which if you sell less, you are less artist than others, risking oblivion.

Physical works can be hidden remaining in artists or collectors' basements, waiting for it to be considered acceptable for "more modern" age.
Digital artwork is timeless in this way, everything is here and now, through reproducibility it can be spread to the world.

However, the massive diffusion of a work does not necessarily protect it from oblivion. What makes the original digital work so important if we can see it everywhere?

Popularity of reproductions, outside the original work, drags its reputation. Regarding the topic just mentioned, there are several collections of NFT art linked to generative artists, very popular even outside the artistic context.
They are not collected only by gallery owners but also by sportsmen, billionaires, influencers, speculators, novice people who get involved in the created hype.
We recognize that precise type of collection even if we don't even remember a single work (there are thousands of them), and we don't know the artists themselves.
In this case we won't see ourselves in front of a work saying "it is a Caravaggio", but we will see ourselves in front of a NFT workart risking just to say "this is that famous NFT" without remembering the artist's name or the collection itself.
These risks are reduced for those who work outside the algorithms and could

boast a form of scarcity in pre-NFT art market days.

The collected works represent the heterogeneity of purposes and procedures of NFT art: some works were born only as a NFT workart, likewise others are photos or scans of physical works collected or collectible in the traditional art market; maybe those physical works were created from a digitally developed draft but not addressed to the NFT market.
Transition of an organic work to digital world is not unique and, first of all, is not just towards one direction.
Starting point in a work development can be digital and/or material while arrival point can be in both markets.

There's plenty fish in the sea...what about
adding a couple more...

Brian Morris, *INSIDERS : S1M2 : Deep*, 4000x4000 px, PNG

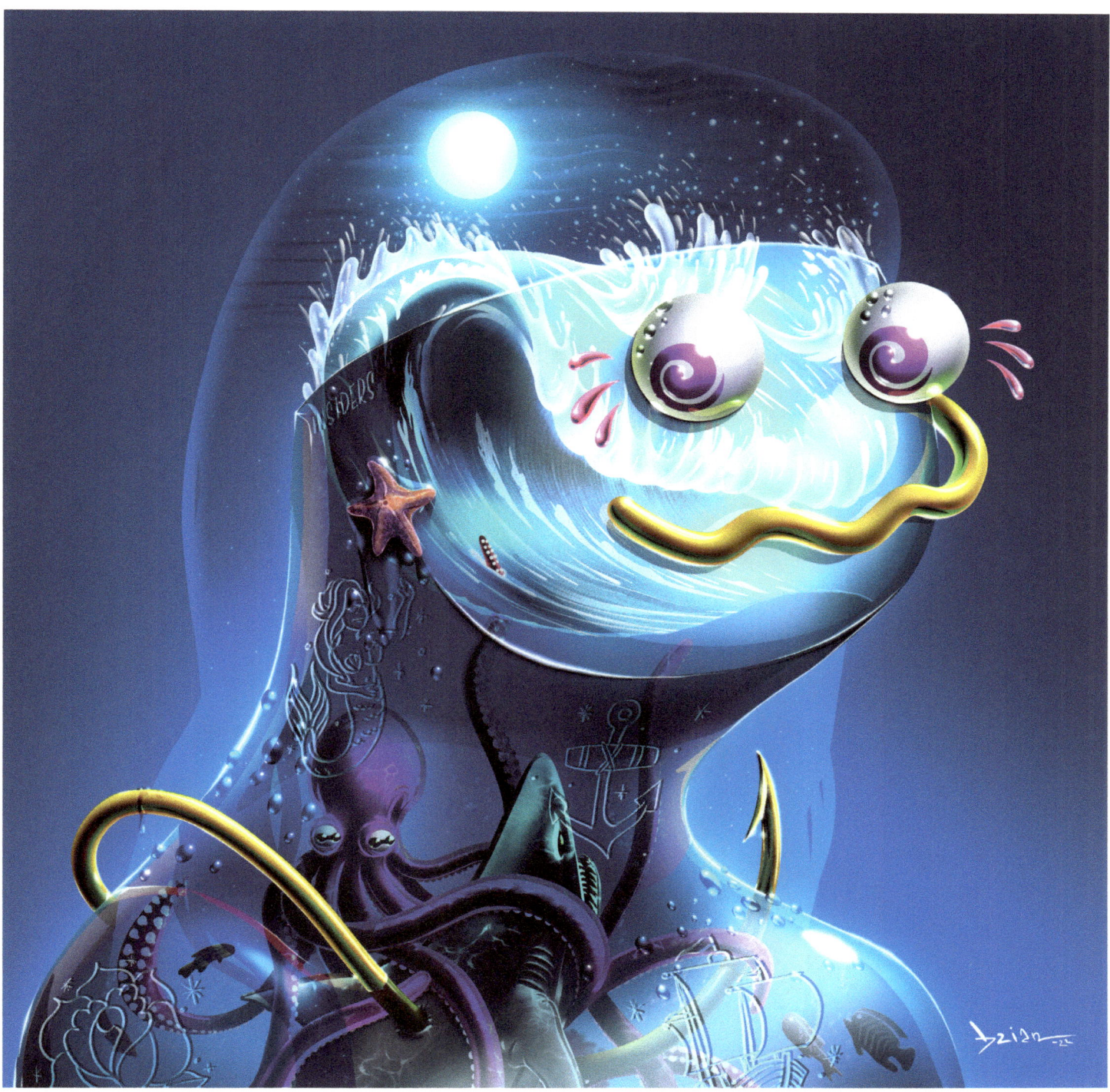

Everyone wears a mask, but you can
finally define who I really am...

Parker Day, *ICONS - X / Malina Stearns*, 3000x4500 px, JPG

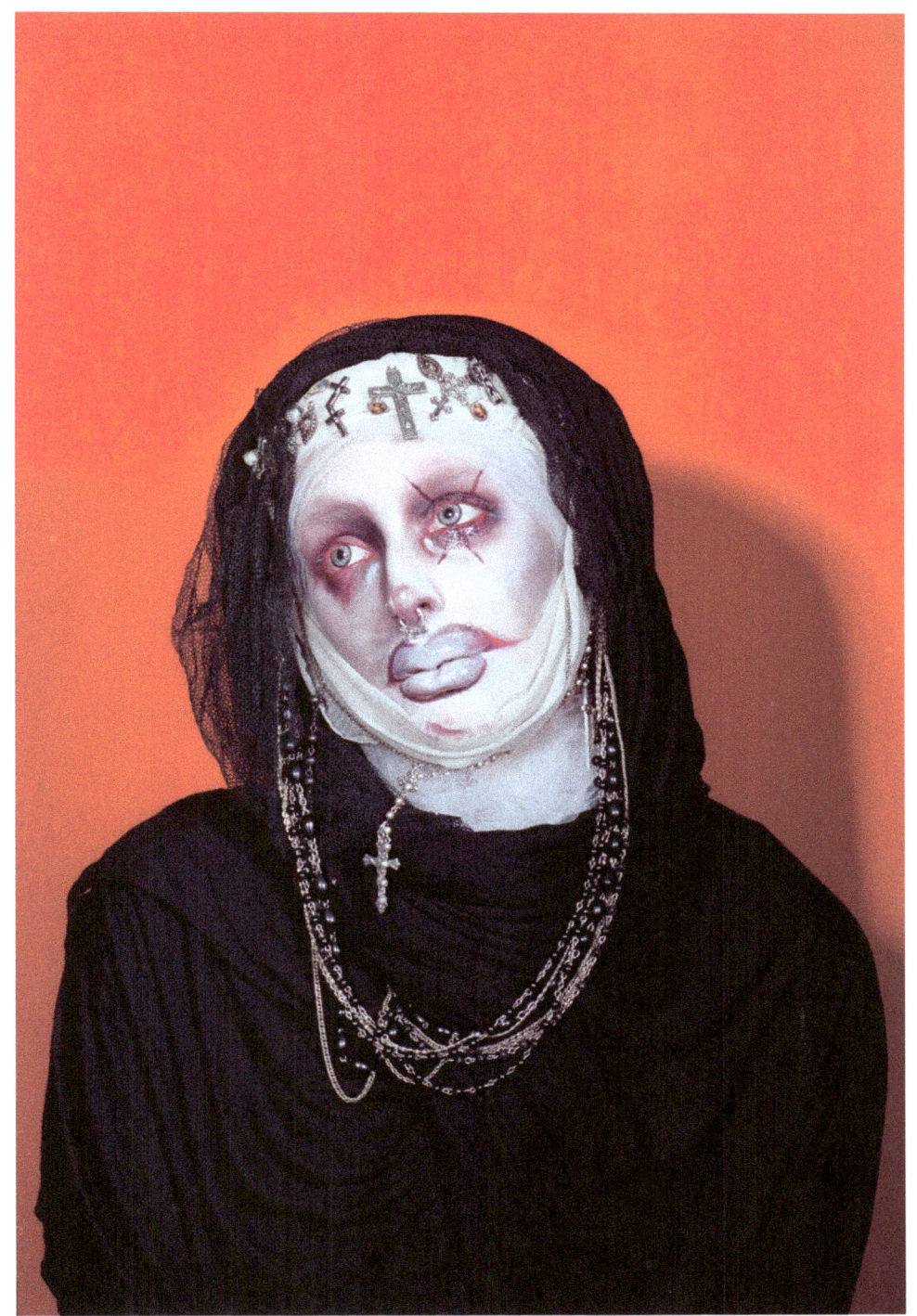

What is the melting point of "this" gold?
(be careful)

Vlad Sopotsko, *#79* | *Gold*, 7936x7936 px, JPG

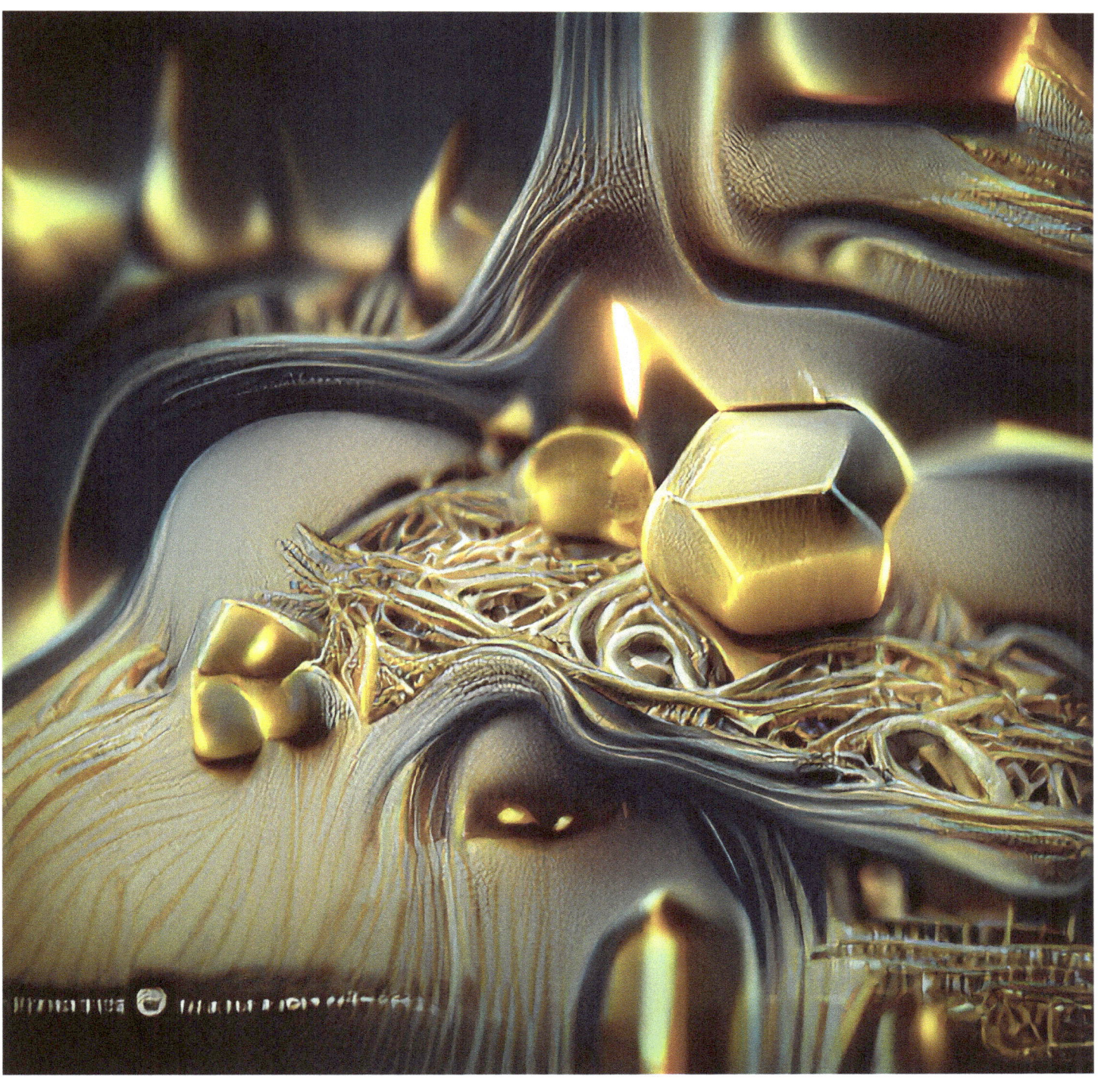

What's in the buckets?

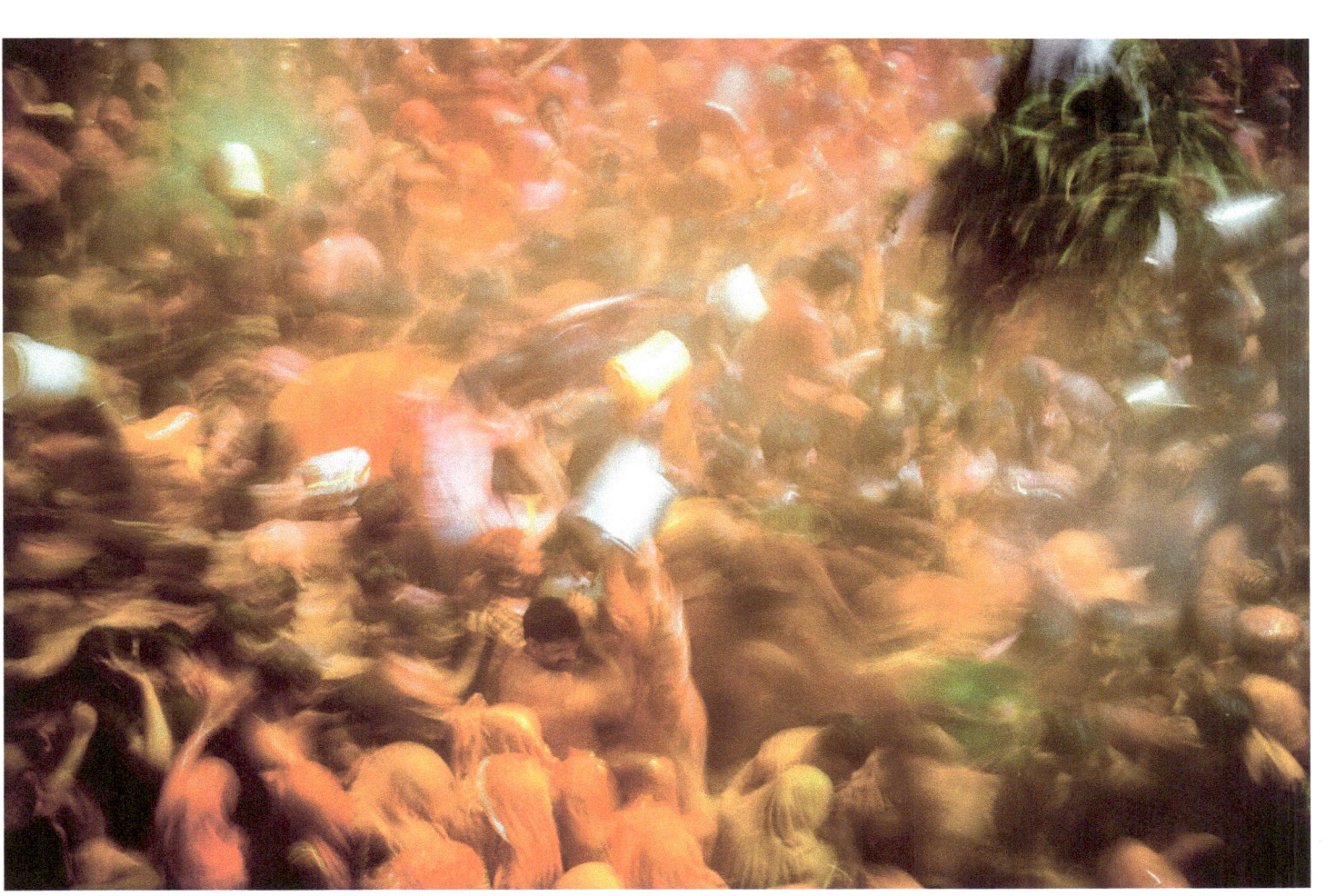

A portal full of creatures...

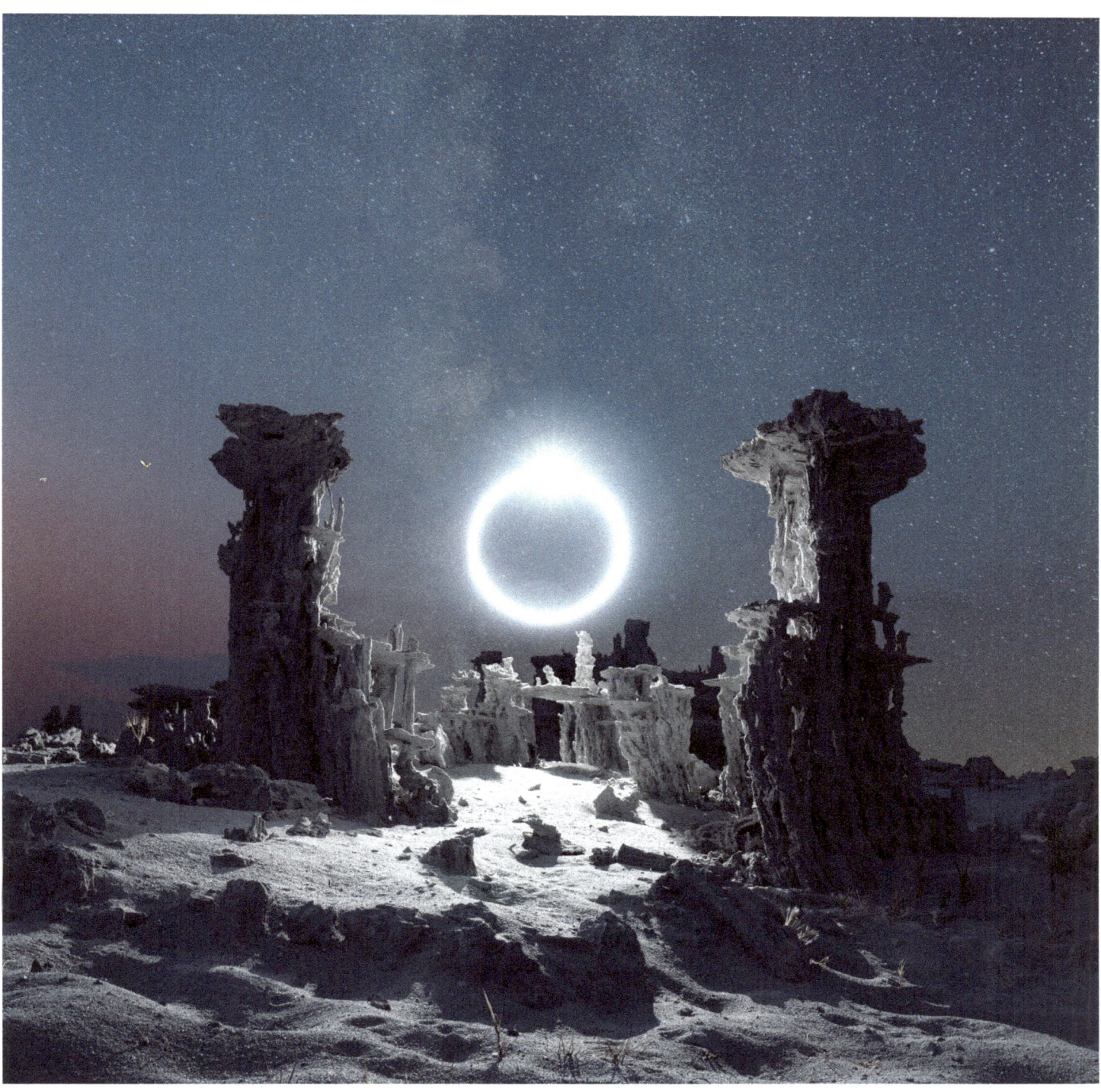

What does this smile hide?

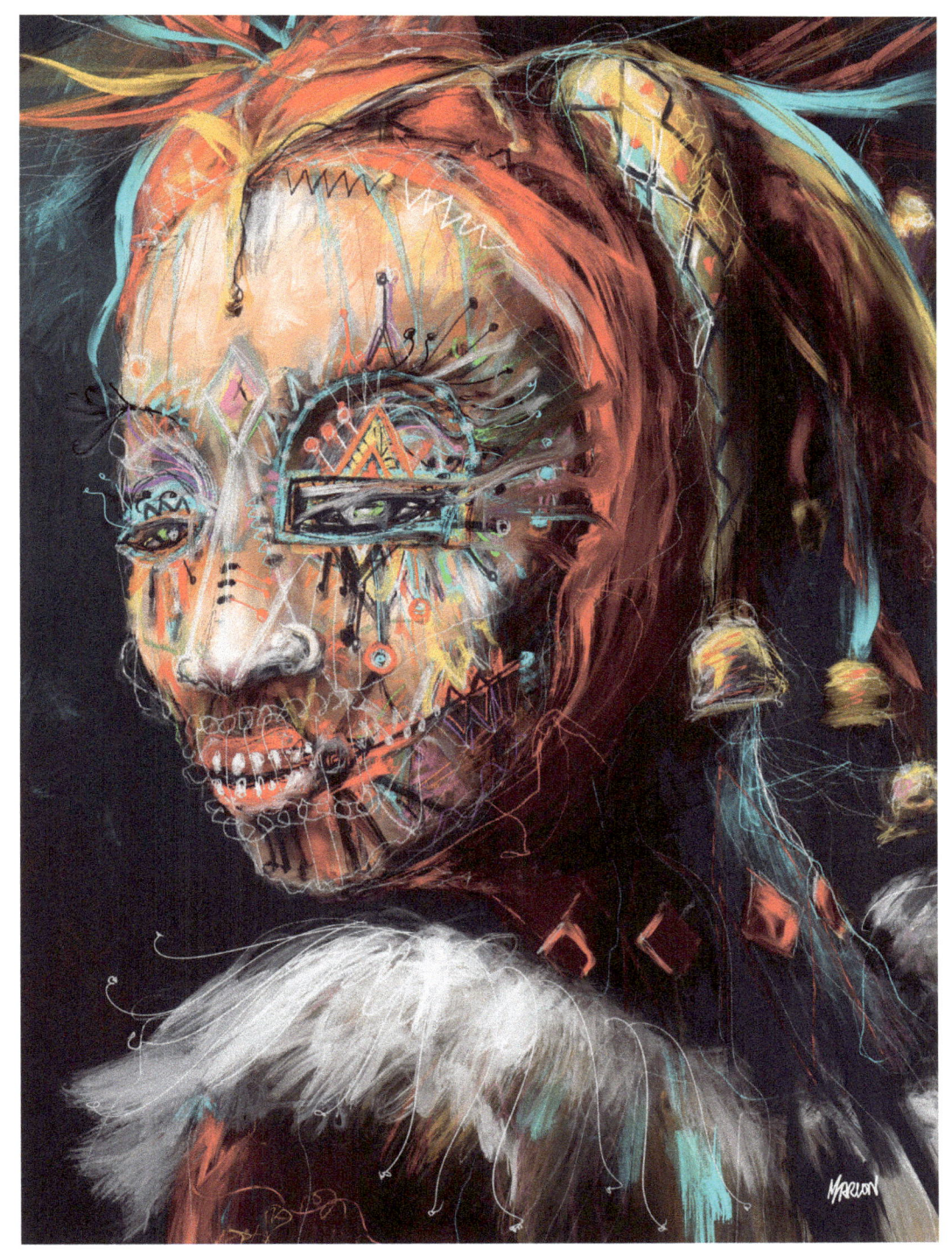

Guess how these leaves were just few
months ago.

Paul Moon, *Remember When We Were Young*, 4000x1871 px, JPG

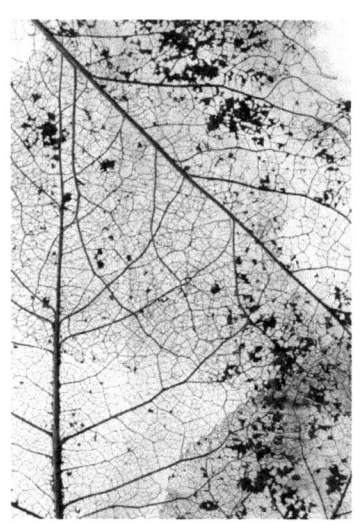 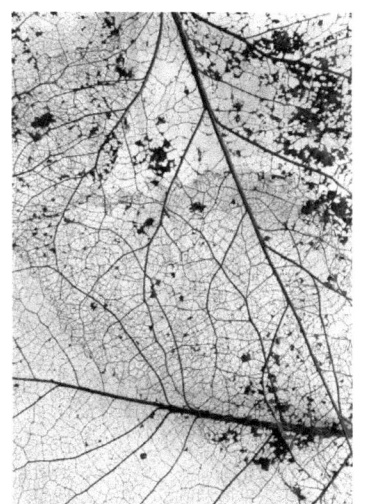 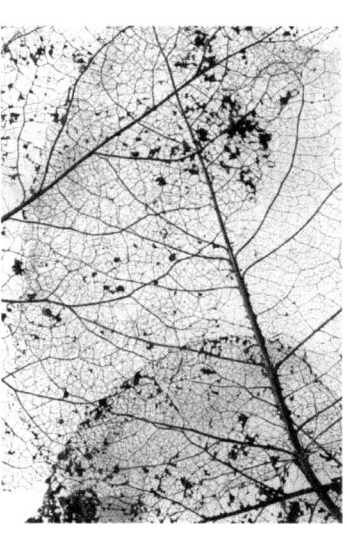

Painting on generative painting...

Michael Reeder, *Cyber Bandit #380*, 2000x2000 px, JPG

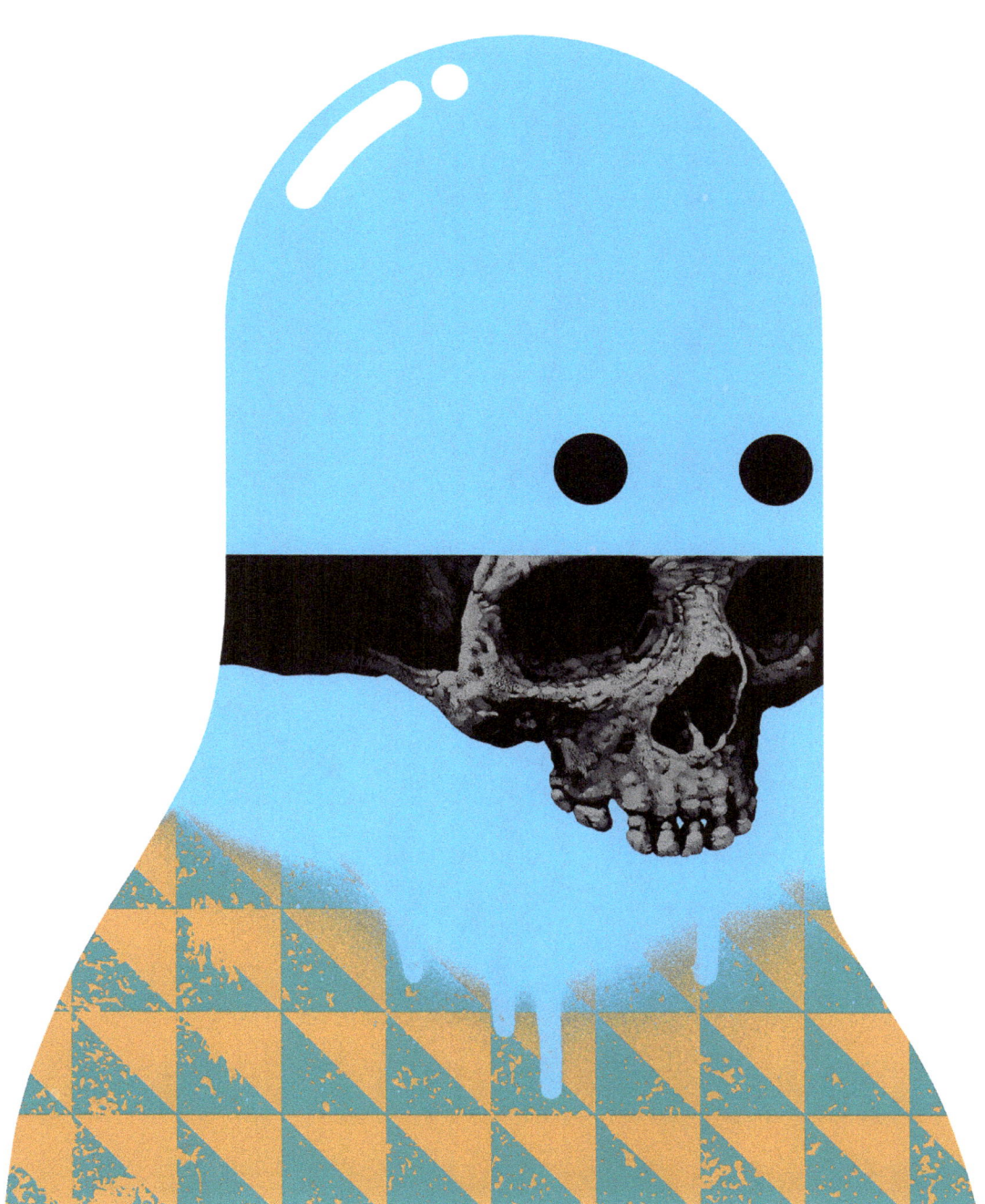

Imagine the metaverse

University of Nicosia, *Fall 2022: BLOC-711*, 4000x4000 px, JPG

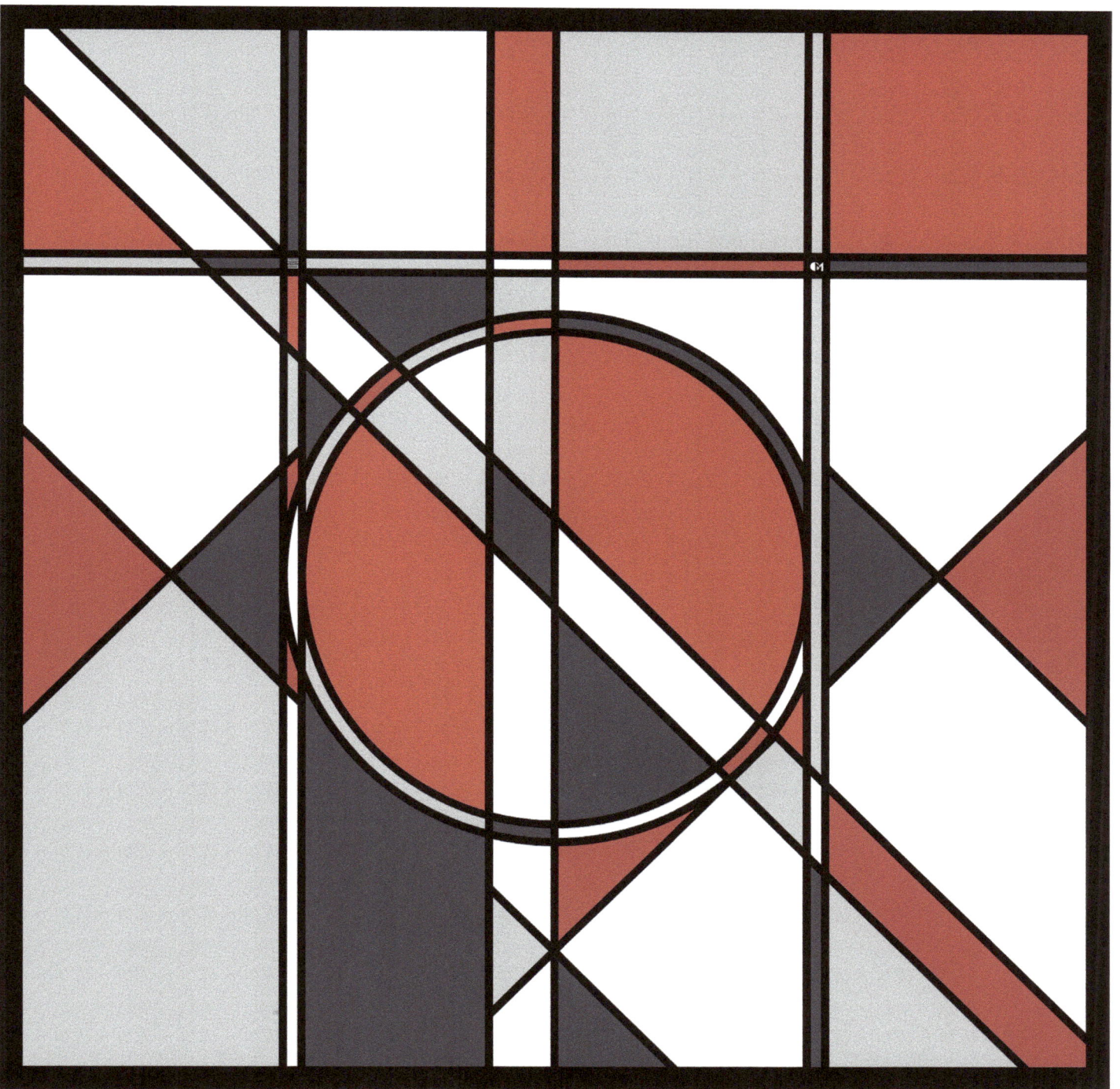

Fill the Otherworld

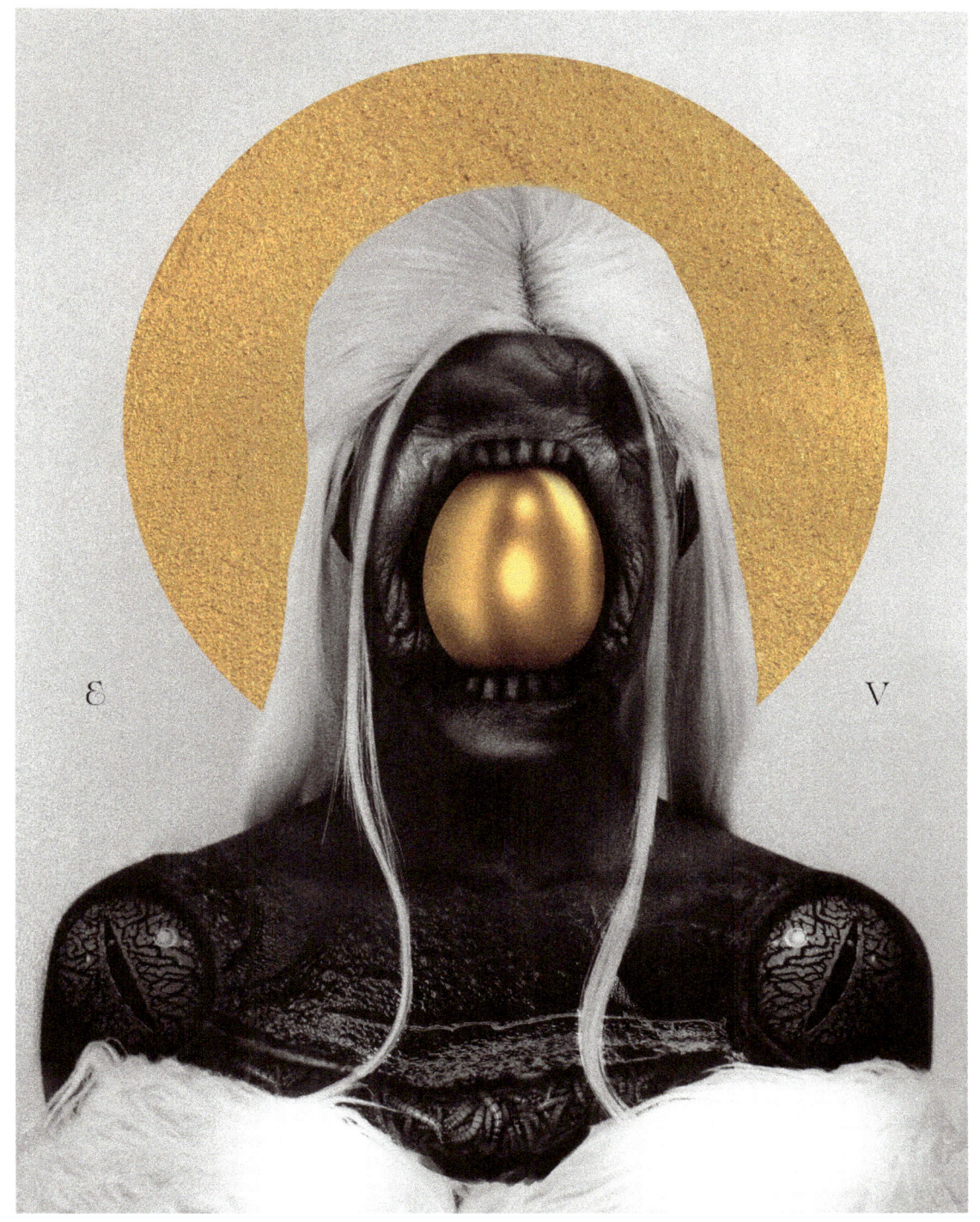

If you could stick a dollar for each day he passed in jail the book would even close?

Pascal Boyart, *Dollars Assange*, 1080x1441 px, JPG

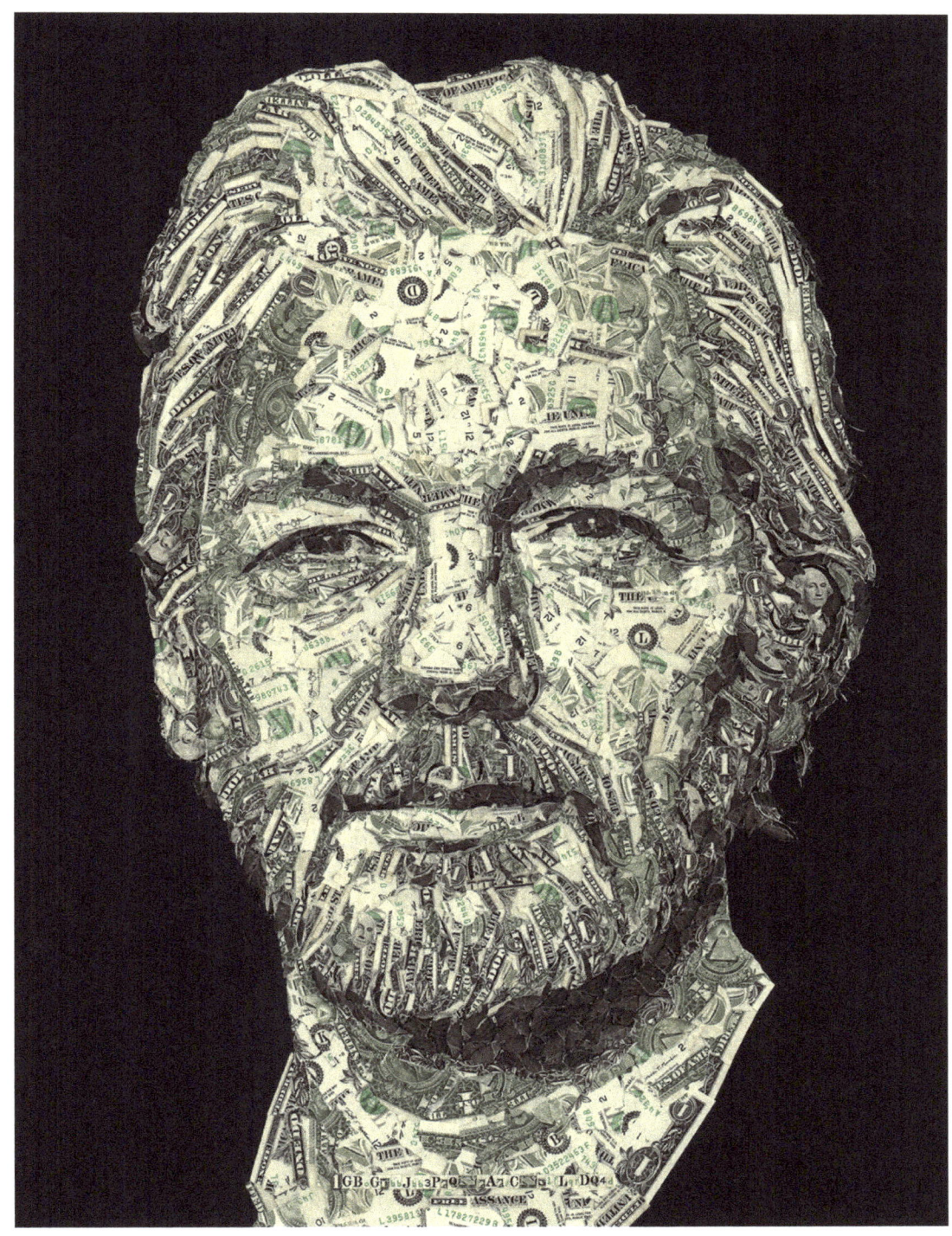

Make it a fine art

TOM LAROC, *HEARD IT ON THE BLOCKCHAIN,* 4000x4000 px, JPG

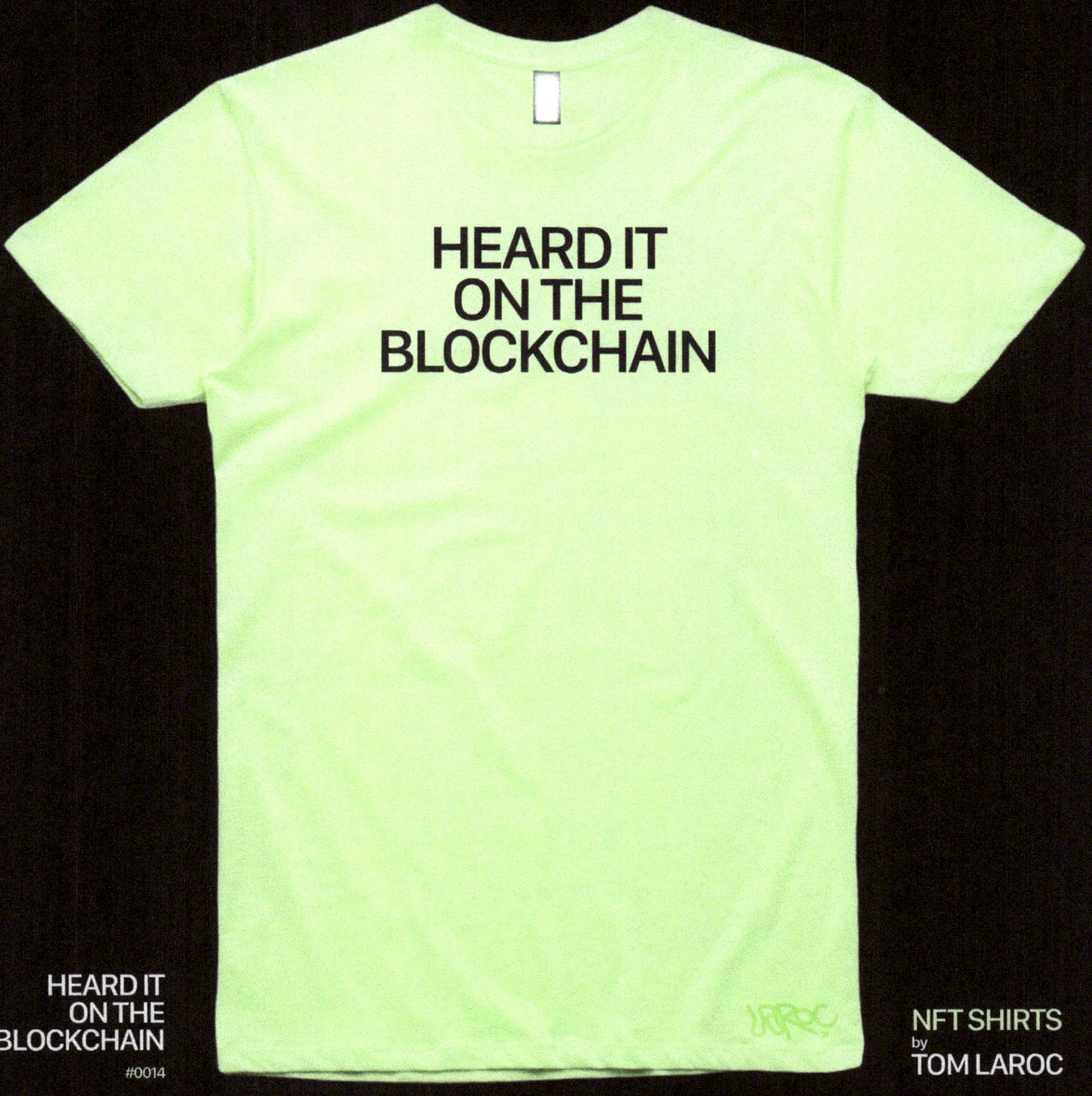

HEARD IT
ON THE
BLOCKCHAIN

HEARD IT
ON THE
BLOCKCHAIN

#0014

NFT SHIRTS
by
TOM LAROC

What would you do to make it suitable for
Instagram?

Alberto Ballocca, *Eseis'*, 3120x4320 px, JPG

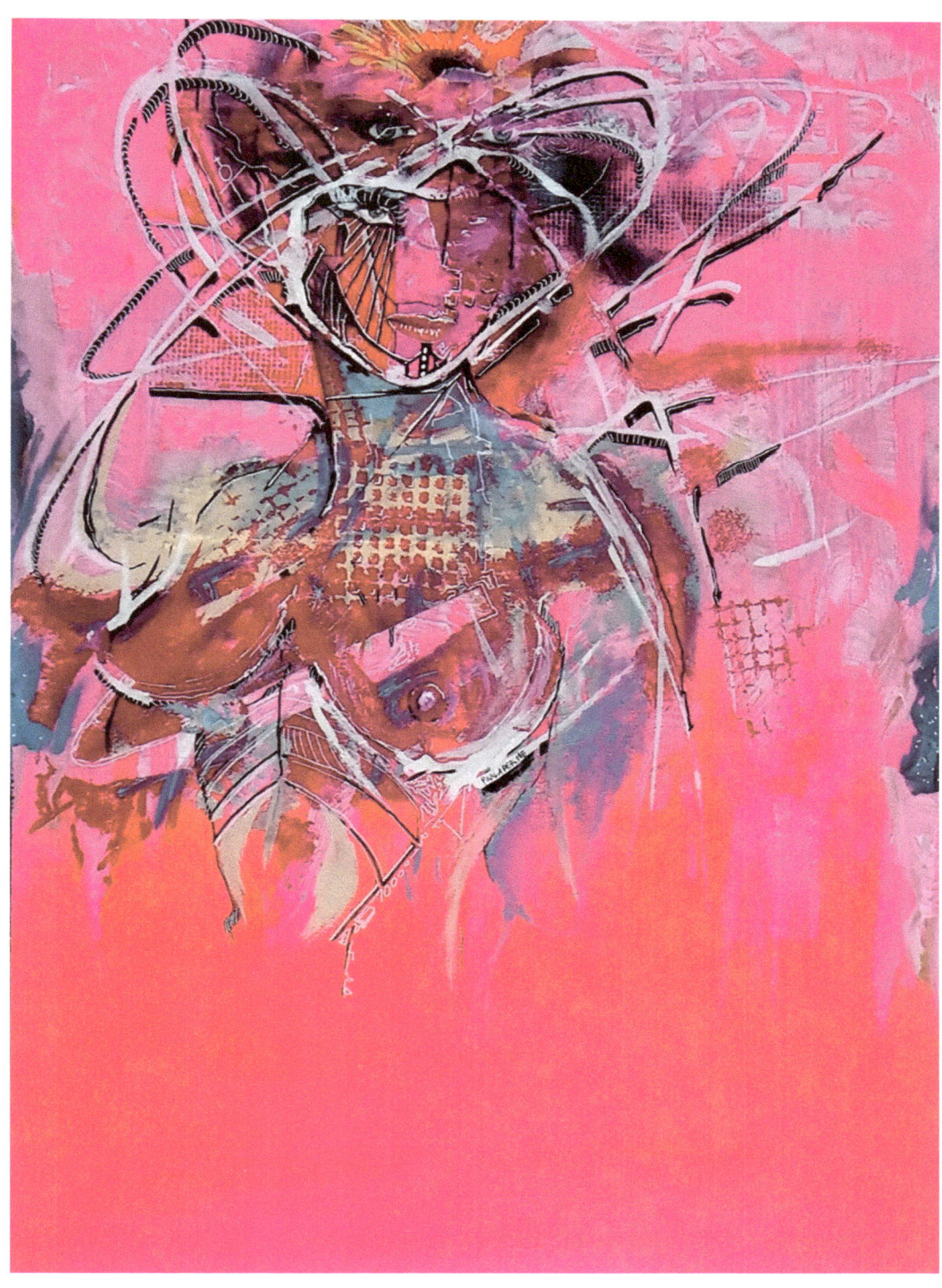

This Ethereal is asking to
become a real kid

Danko, *ETHEREALS #48*, 5000x5000 px, JPG

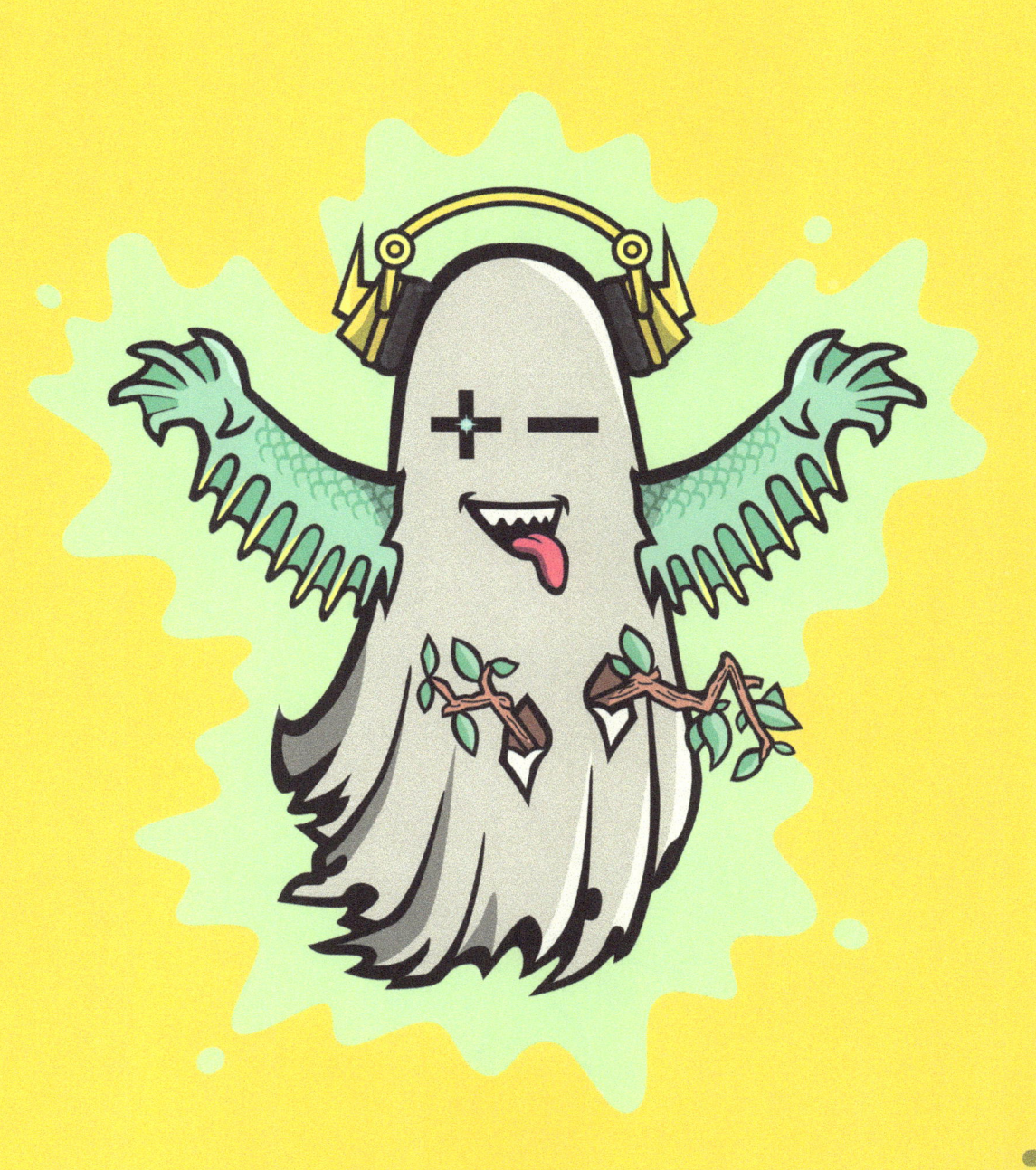

Uncensored

Jose Lopez Vergara, *Poor Little Devil*, 3900x5221 px, JPG

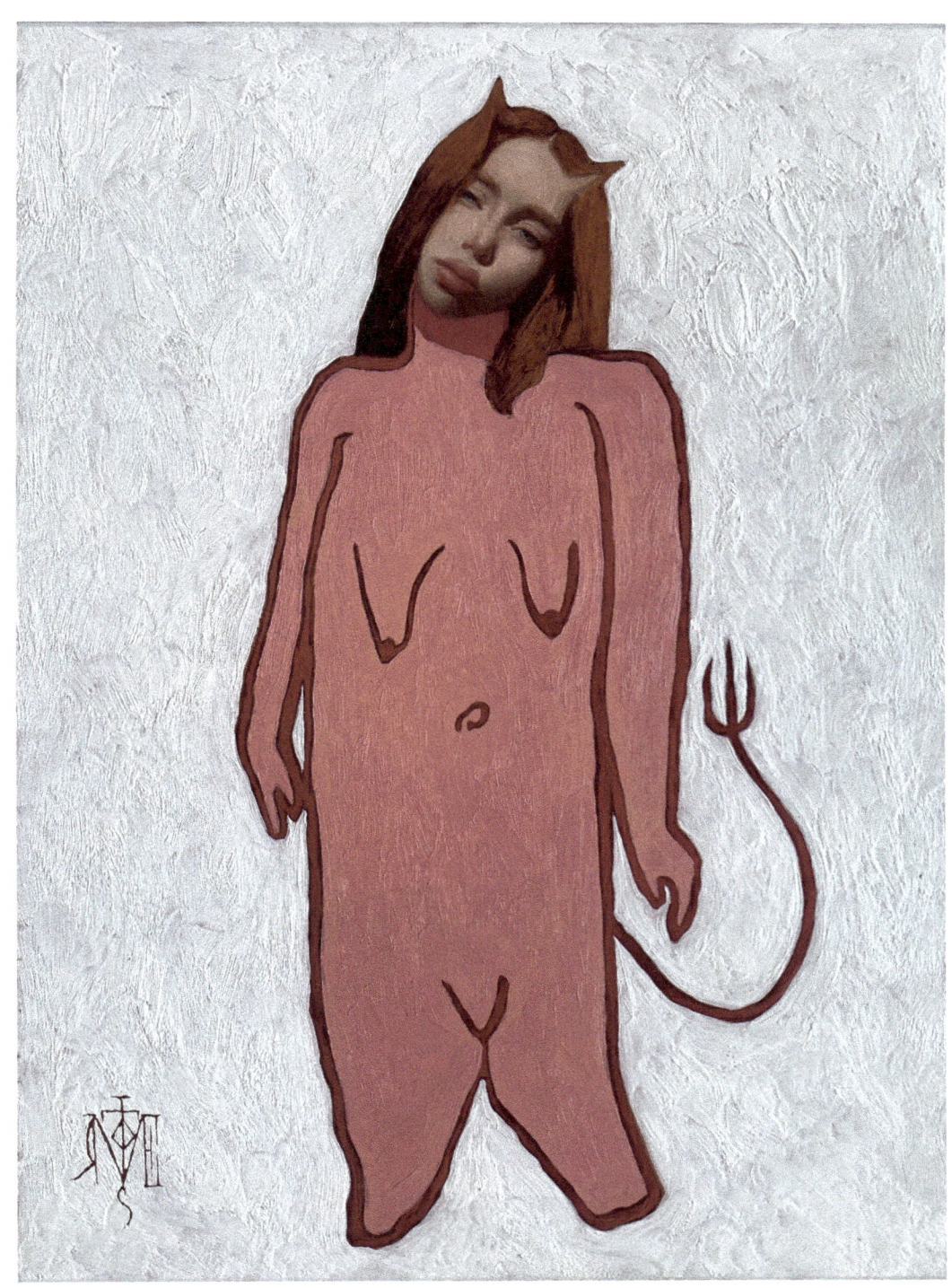

Hang it

-

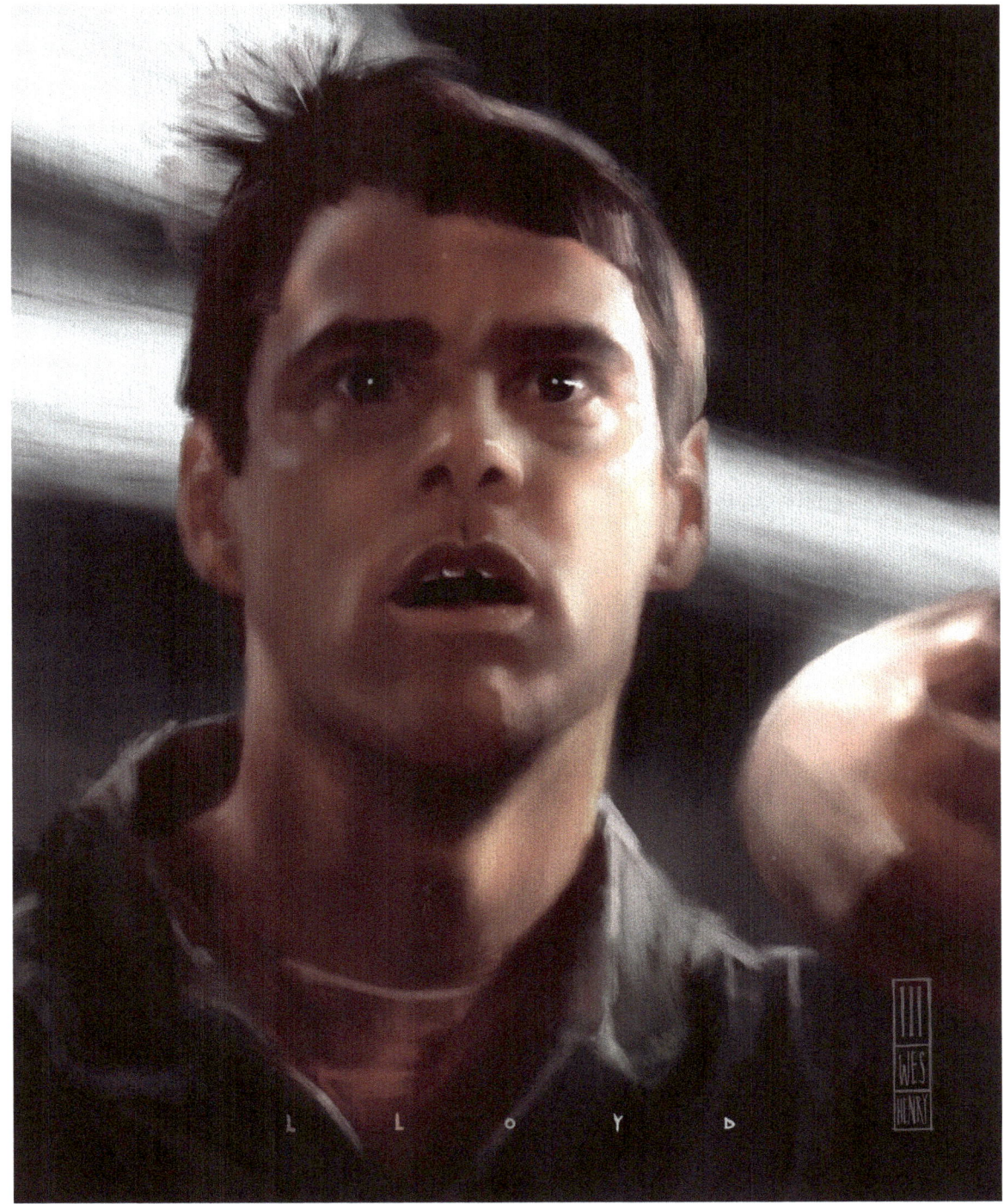

LLOYD

This is coloring book material

Olive47, *The Mushroom People 0089,* 3000x3000 px, PNG

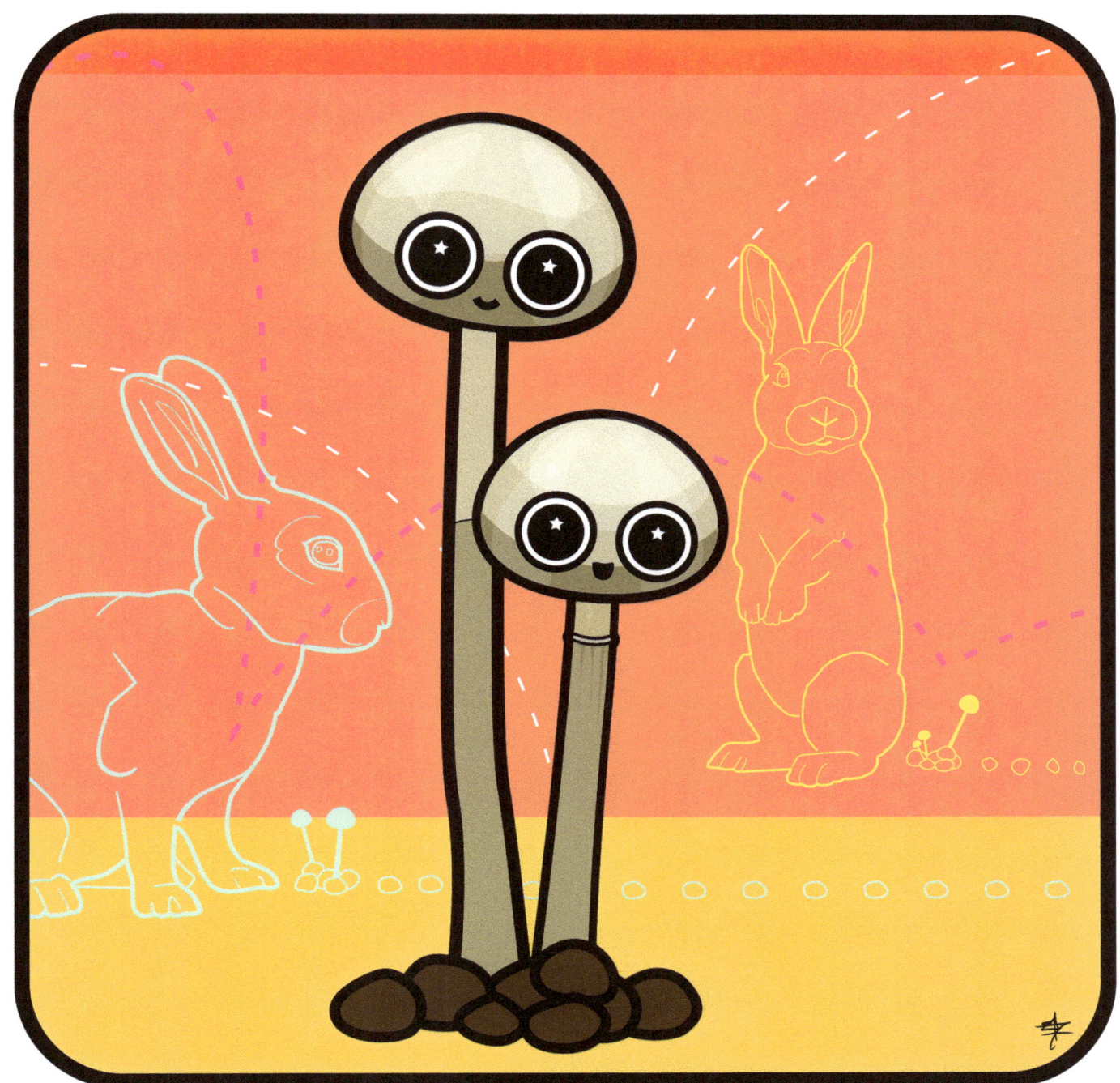

What does it arose,? Write it down

Hugo Faz, *STRICKEN*, 3848x5772 px, JPG, Contract info at https://etherscan.io/nft/0xBd2A76324bf2c093D9 15d4838F099724005bf181/6

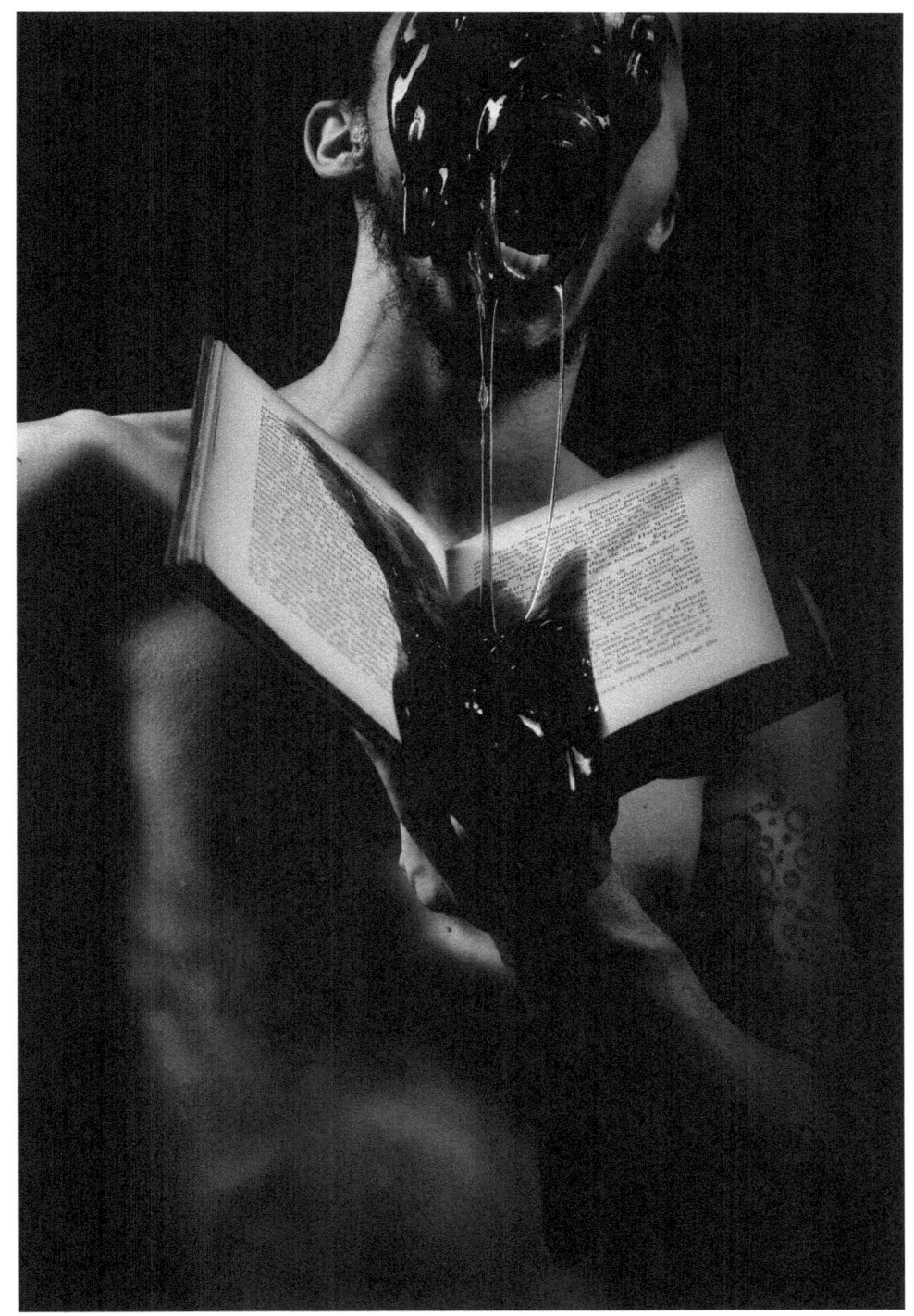

Guide your hand as an artist

Ian Jones, *ScribbleGlitch #9,* 3000x3000 px, JPG

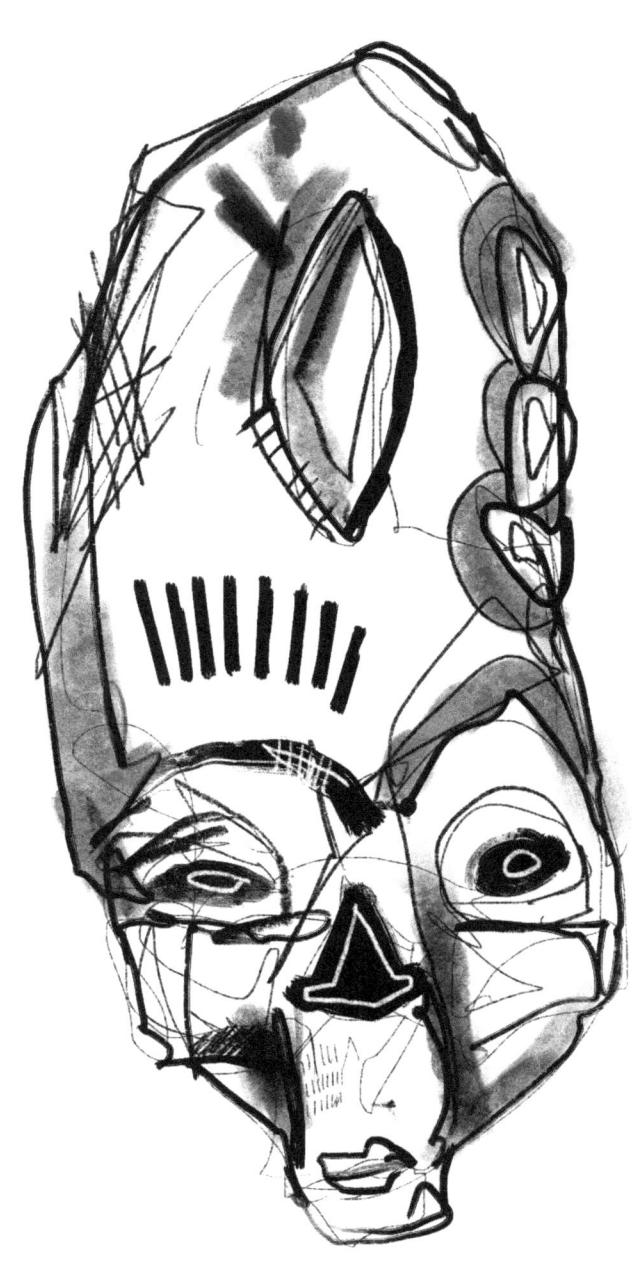

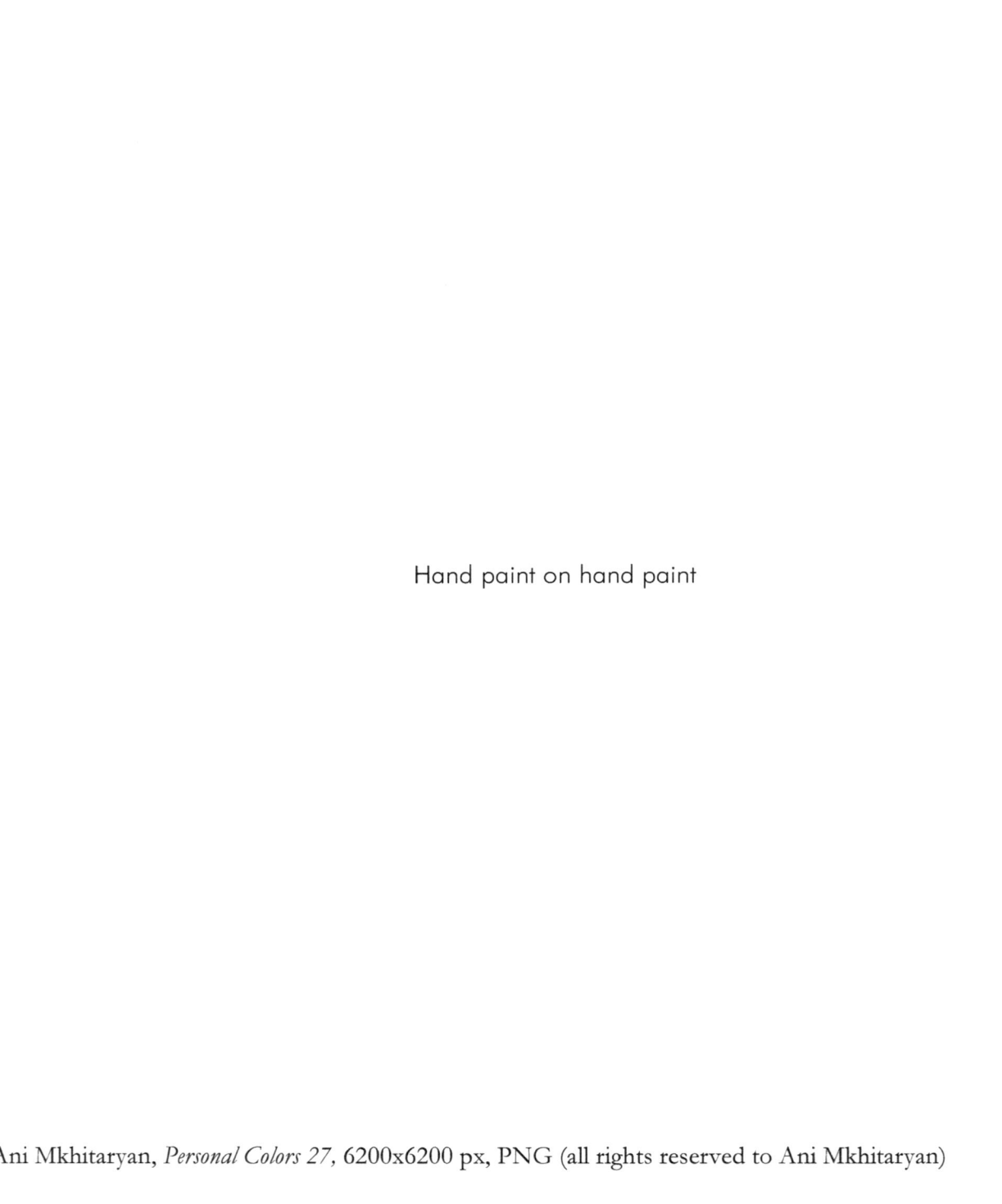

Hand paint on hand paint

Ani Mkhitaryan, *Personal Colors 27*, 6200x6200 px, PNG (all rights reserved to Ani Mkhitaryan)

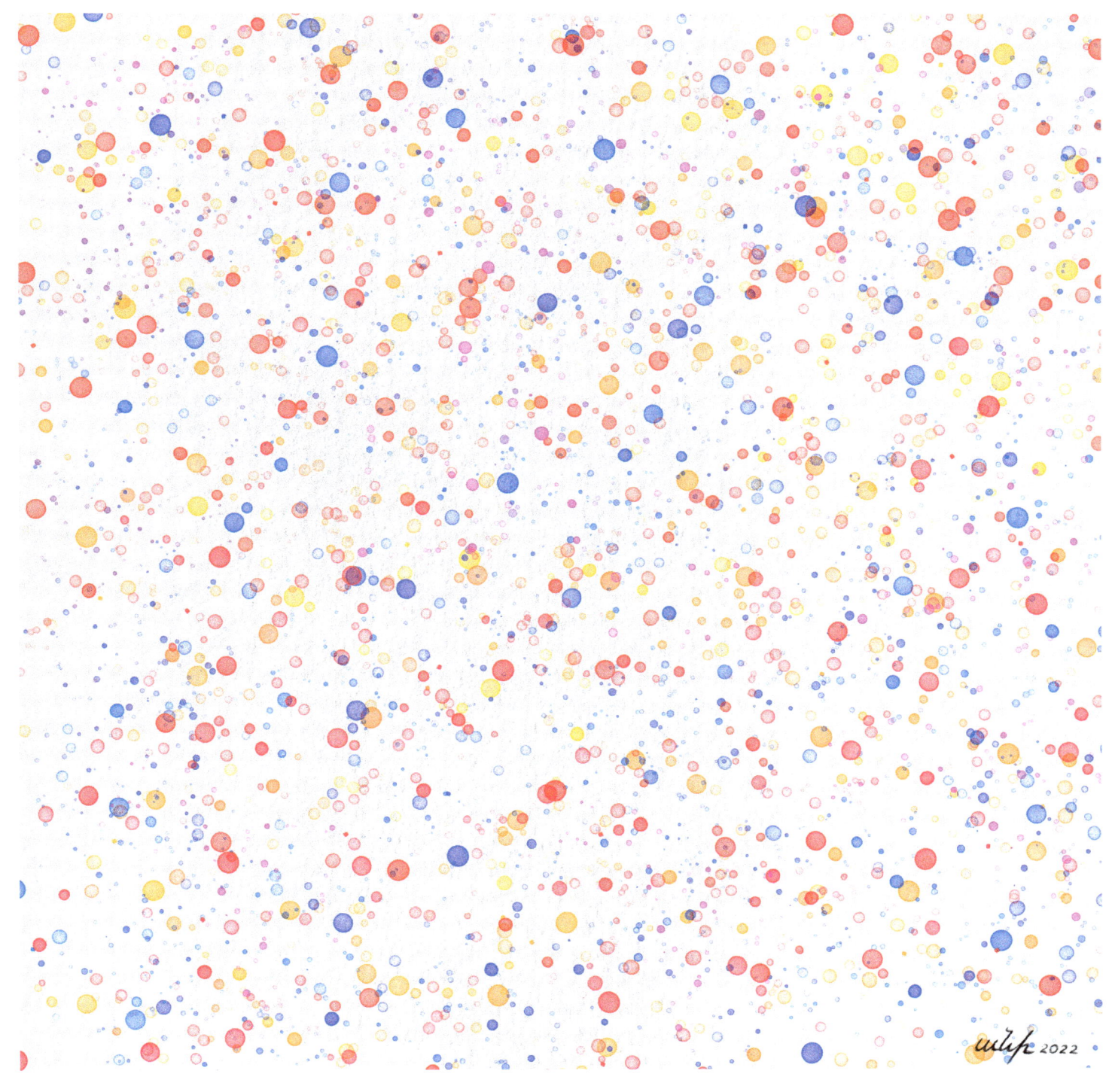

Your head is already full

Jason Balducci, *French Windows*, 1000x1000 px, PNG

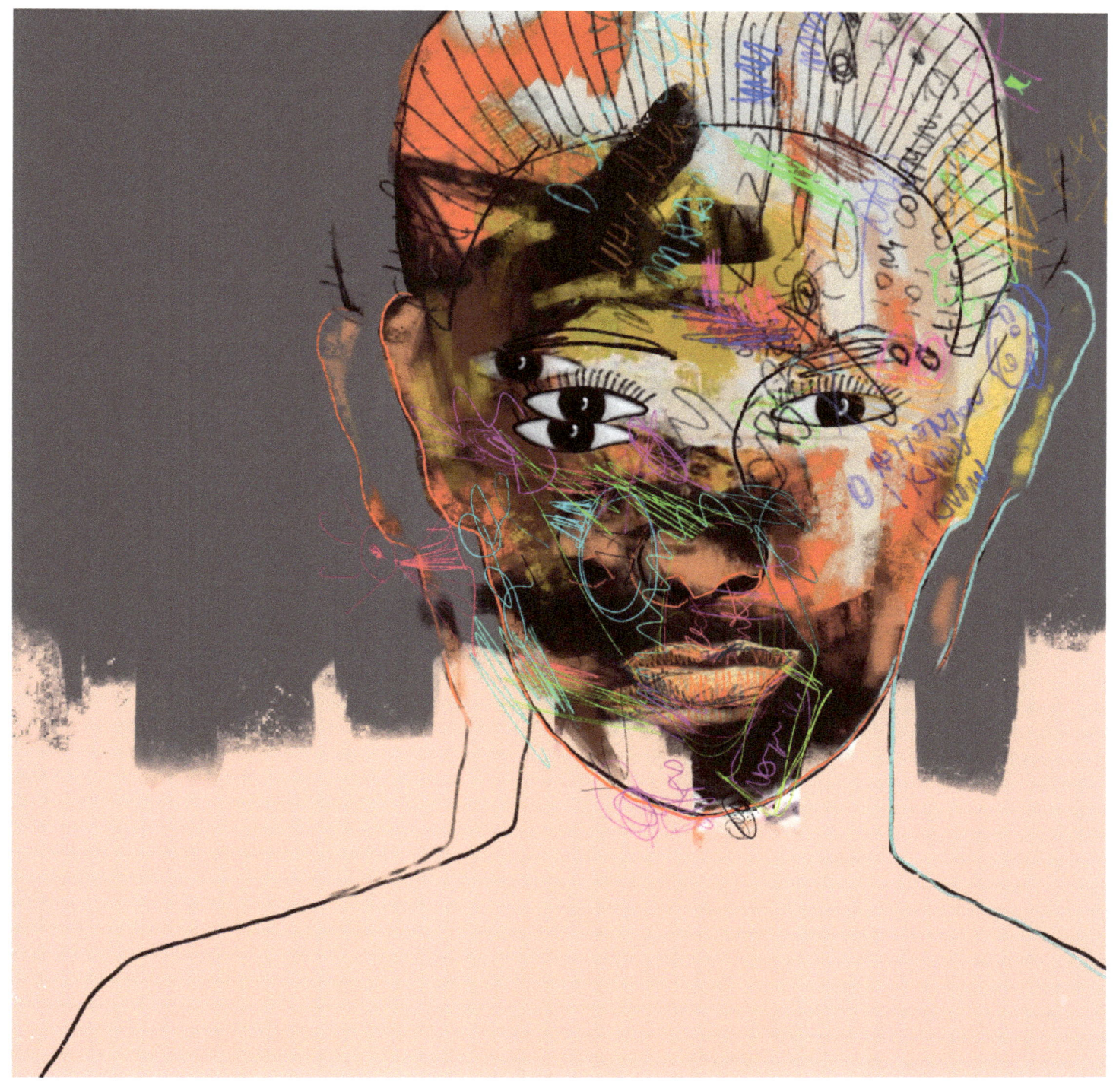

In need of company...

Neil Burnell, *Fireworks*, 4000x2670 px, JPG

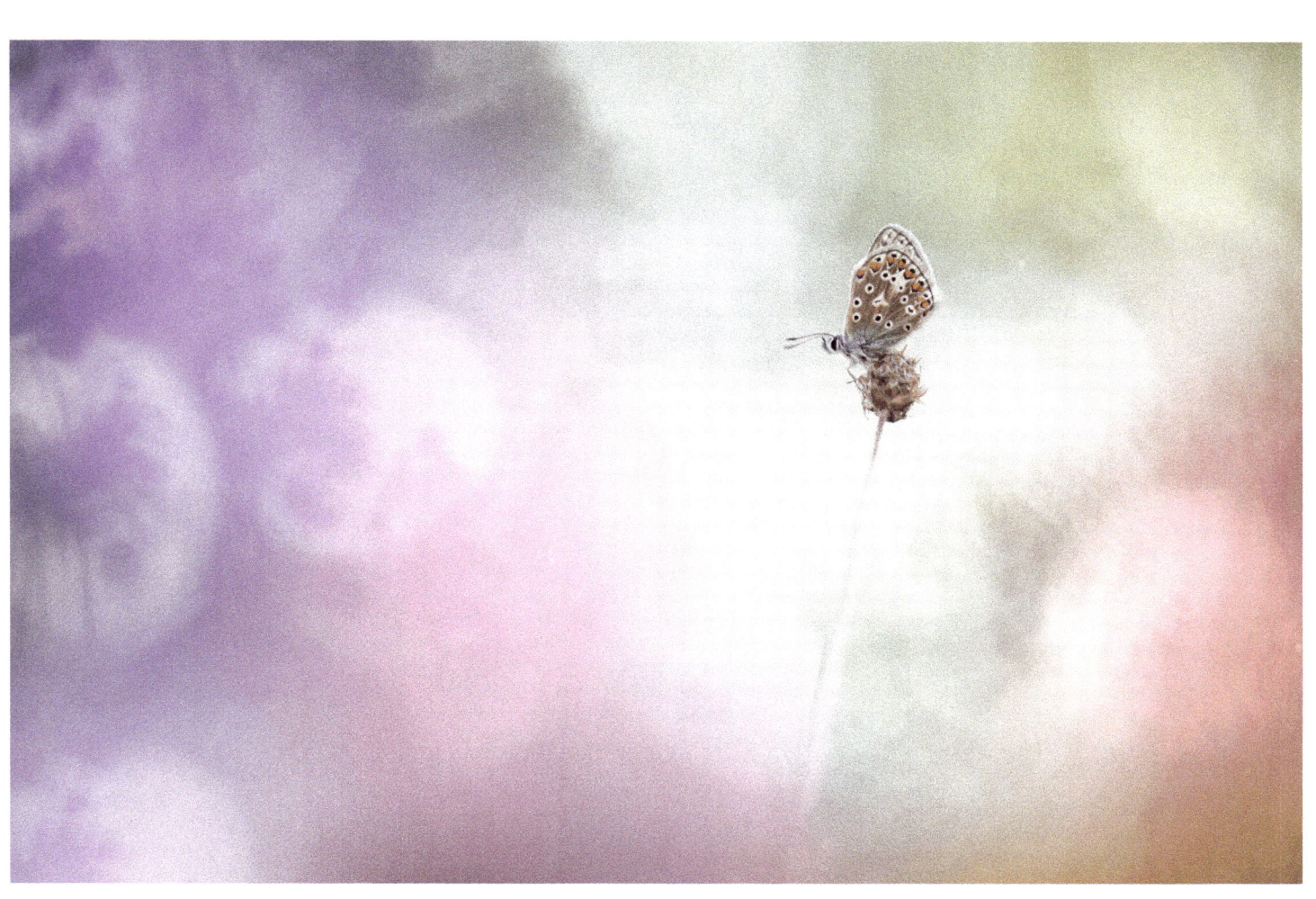

Fill the blank space

JPLans, *The Travelers*, 3582x4838, JPG

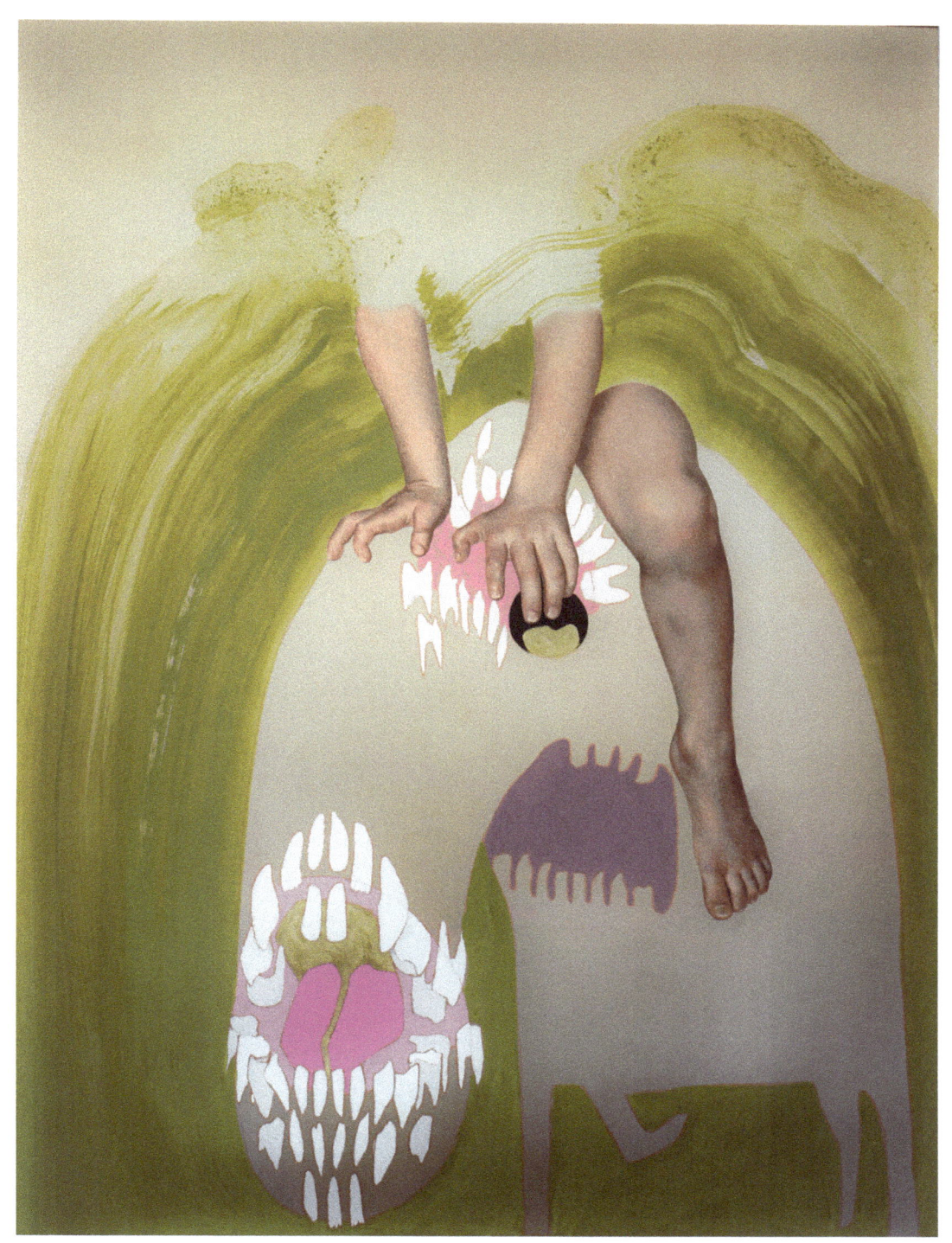

Feed the void

Nate Bear, *Free Ride,* 4000x5000 px, JPG

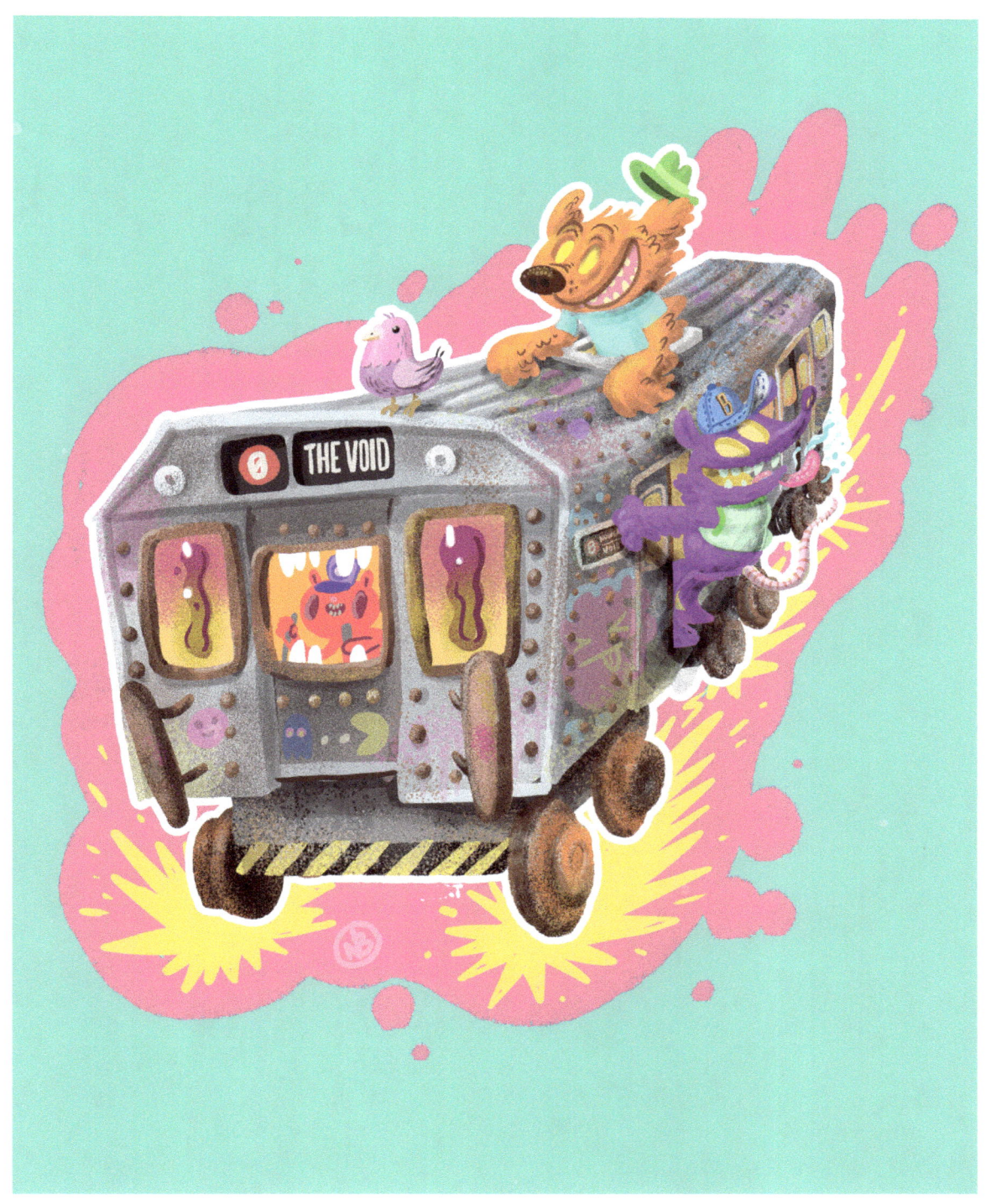

Eyes are windows to the soul

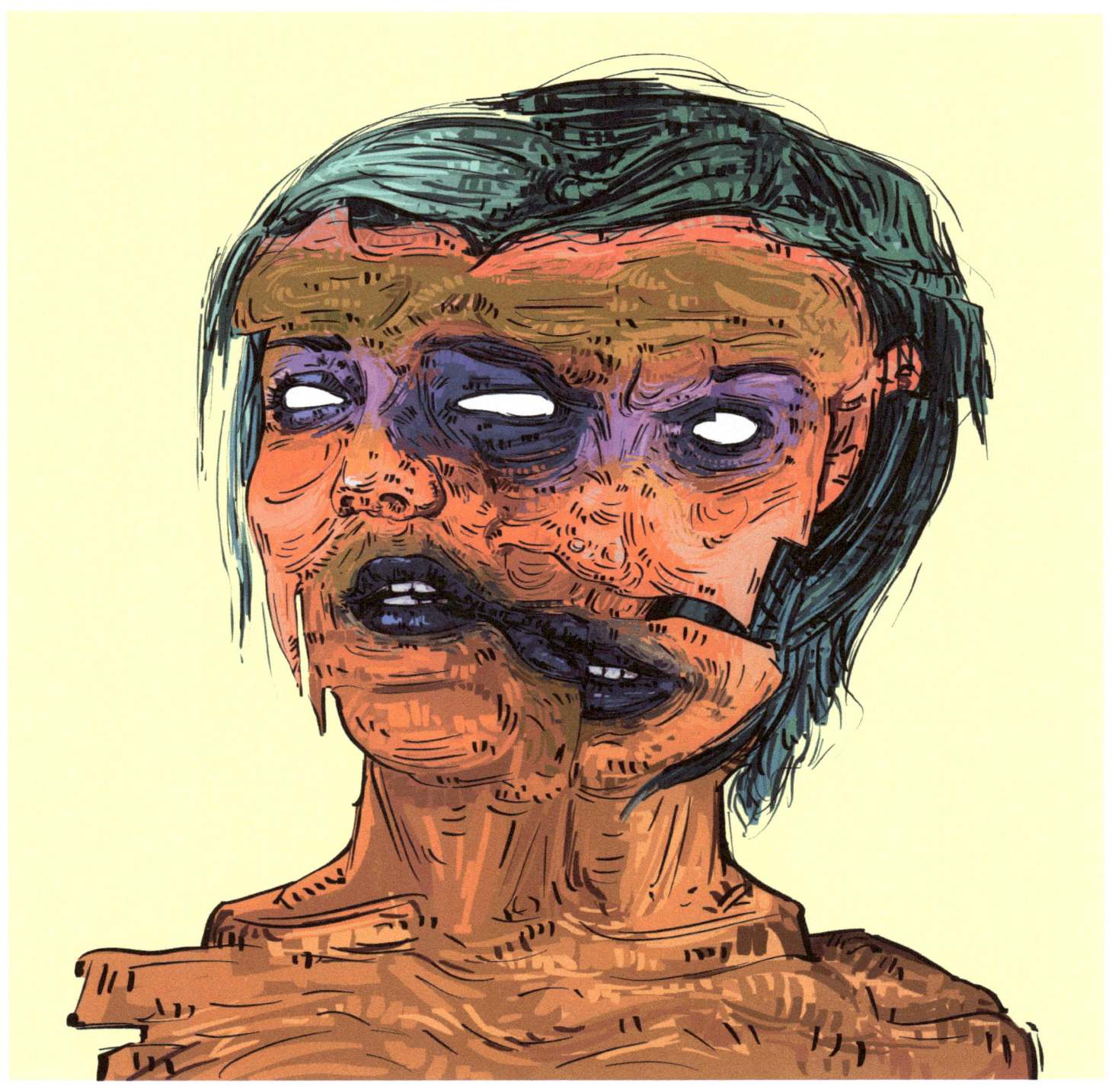

Something like a trompe l'oeil would fit
well

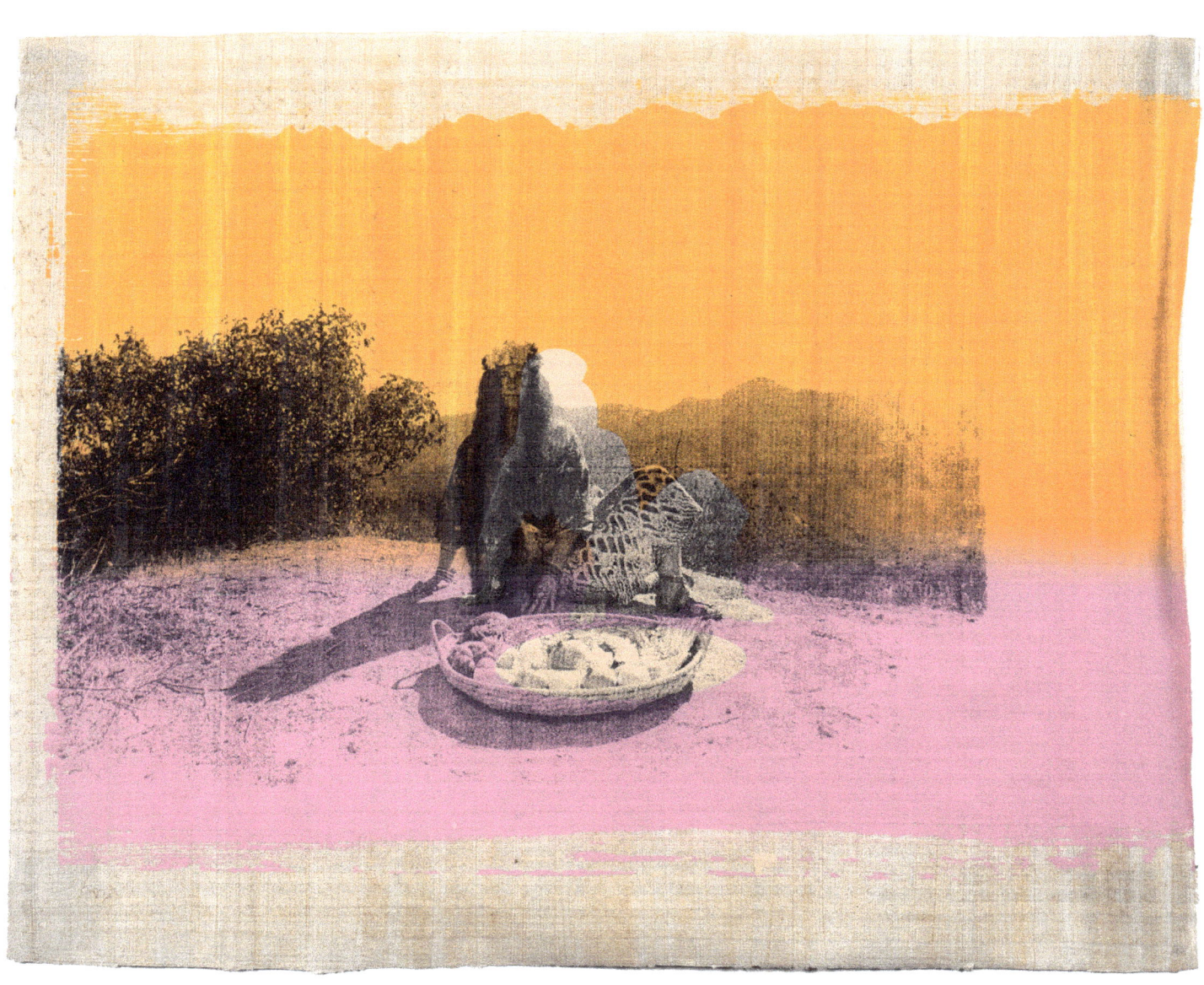

Design something in 3D

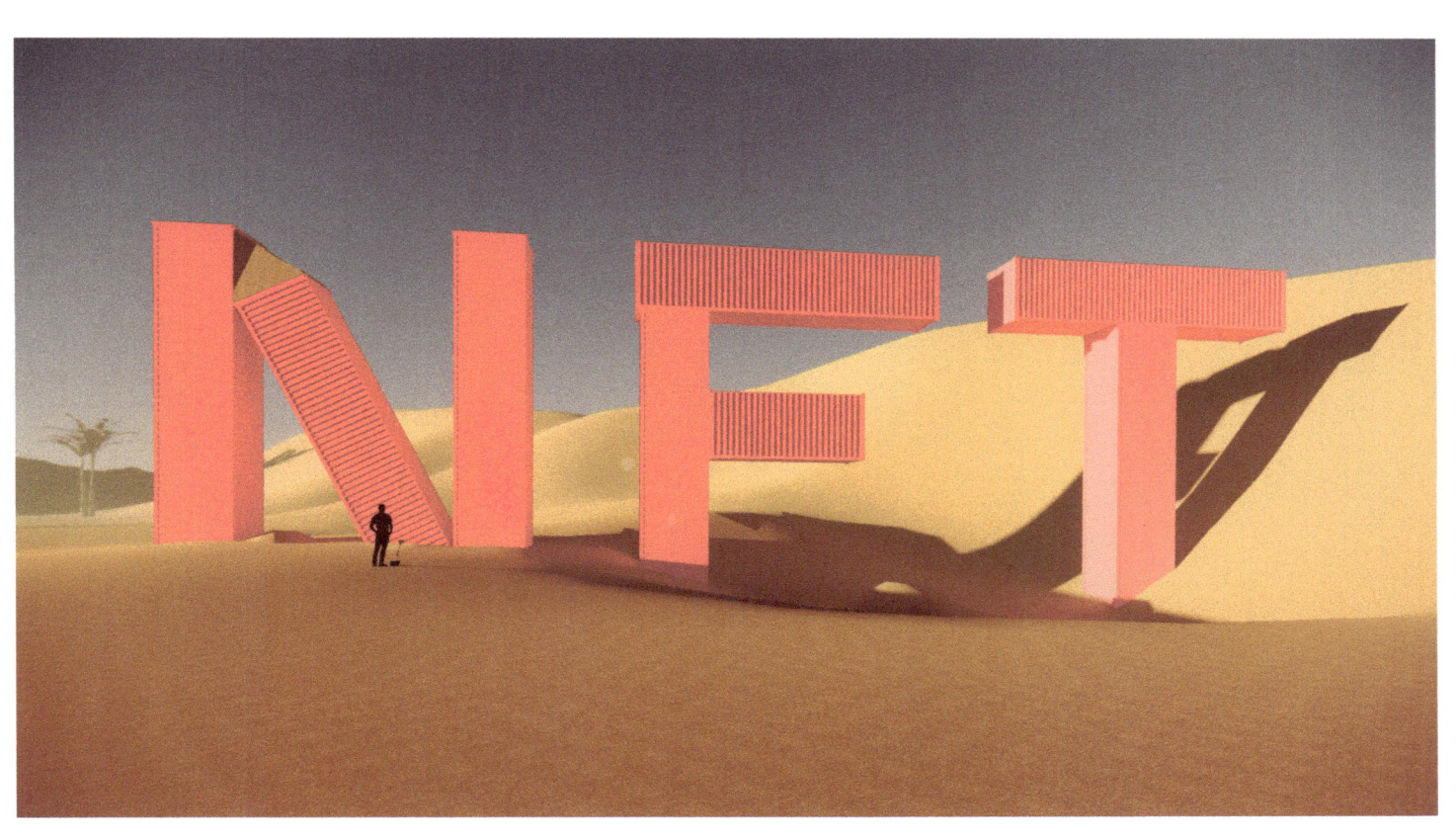

Write a poem...

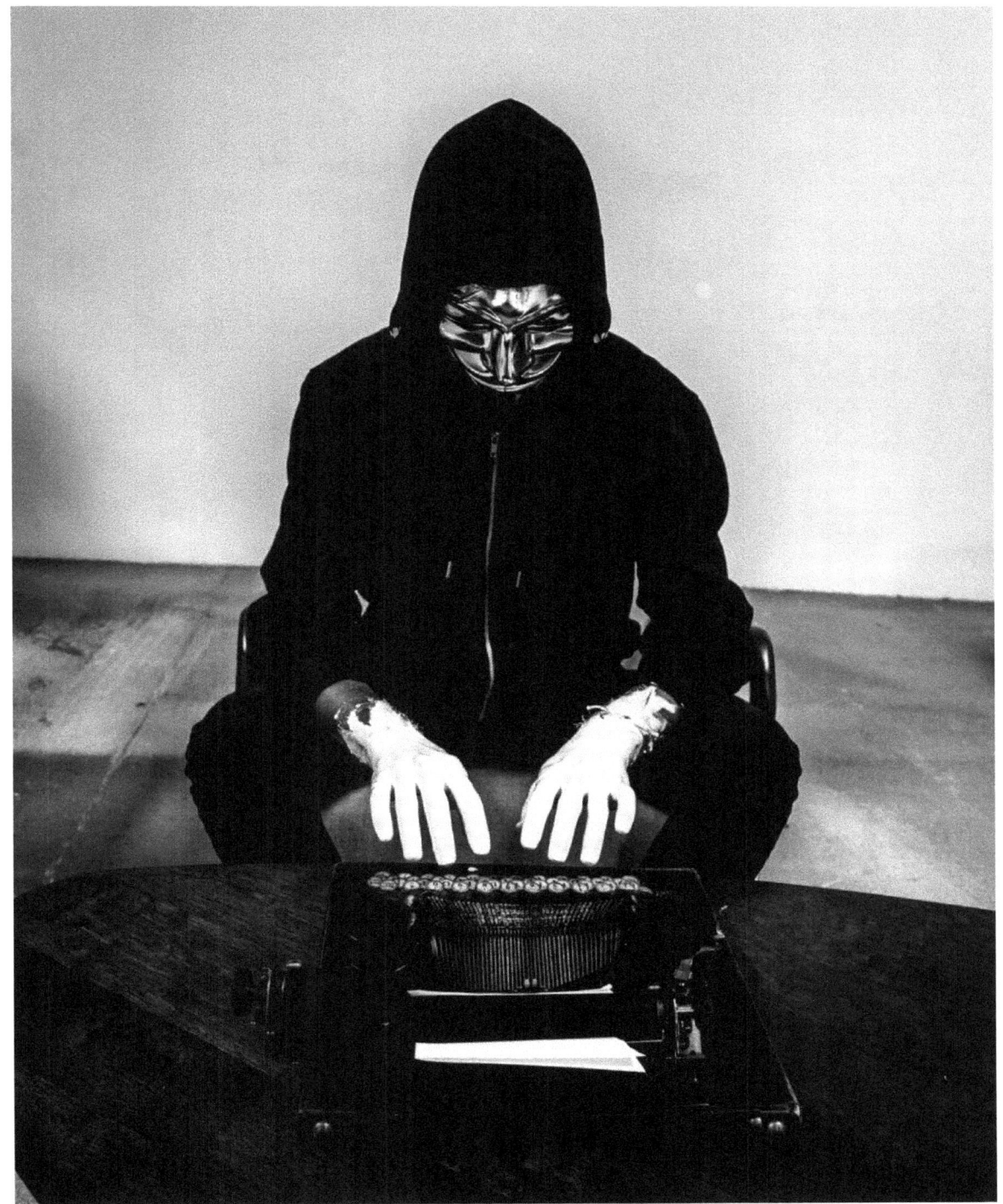

Change a word

Mike Mongo, *I AM REALLY JUST INTO YOU,* 4000x4000 px, PNG

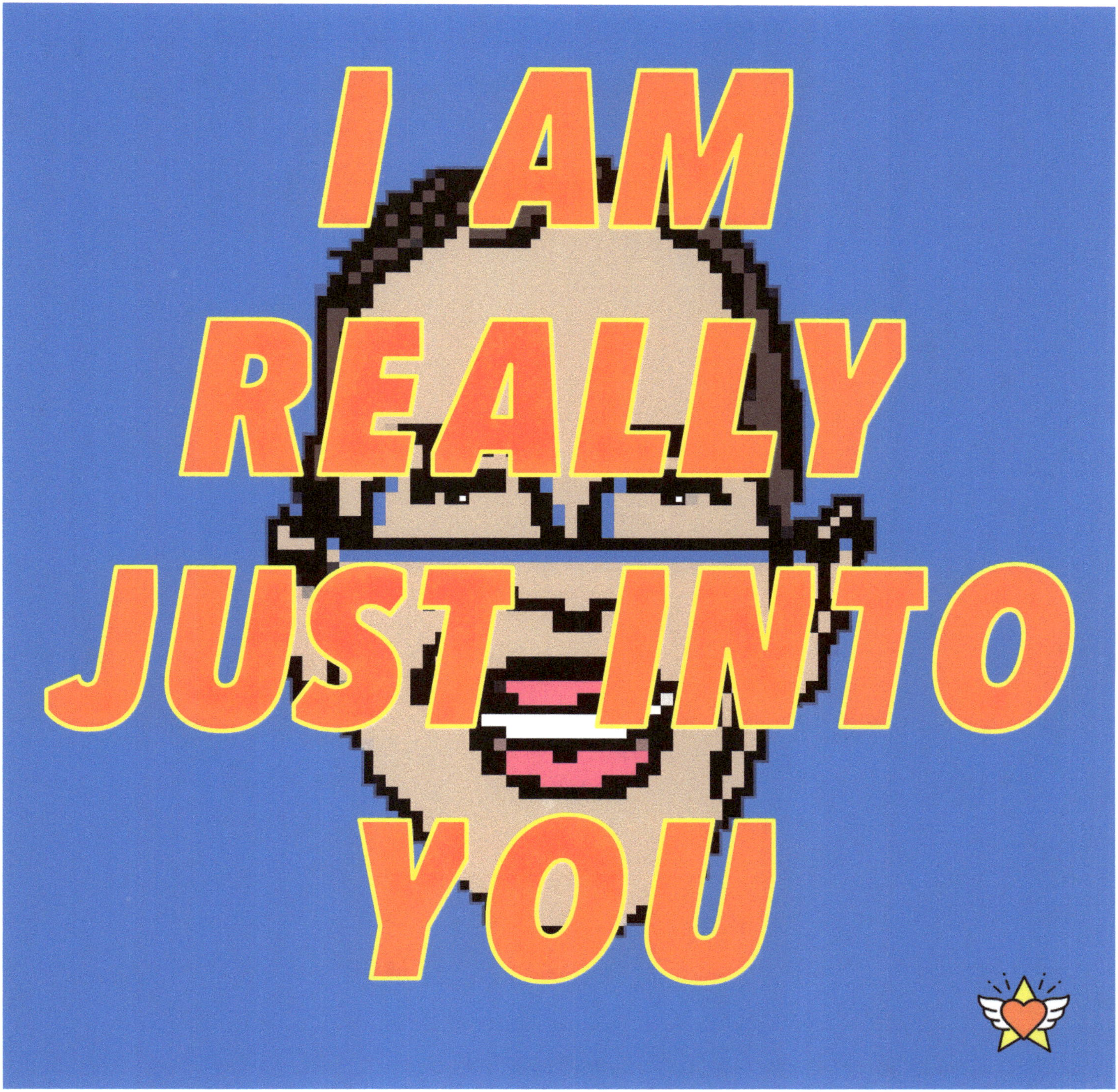

Expand this unreal reality

Marco Signorini, *"Untitled" from the series Anagram,* 846x846 px, JPG

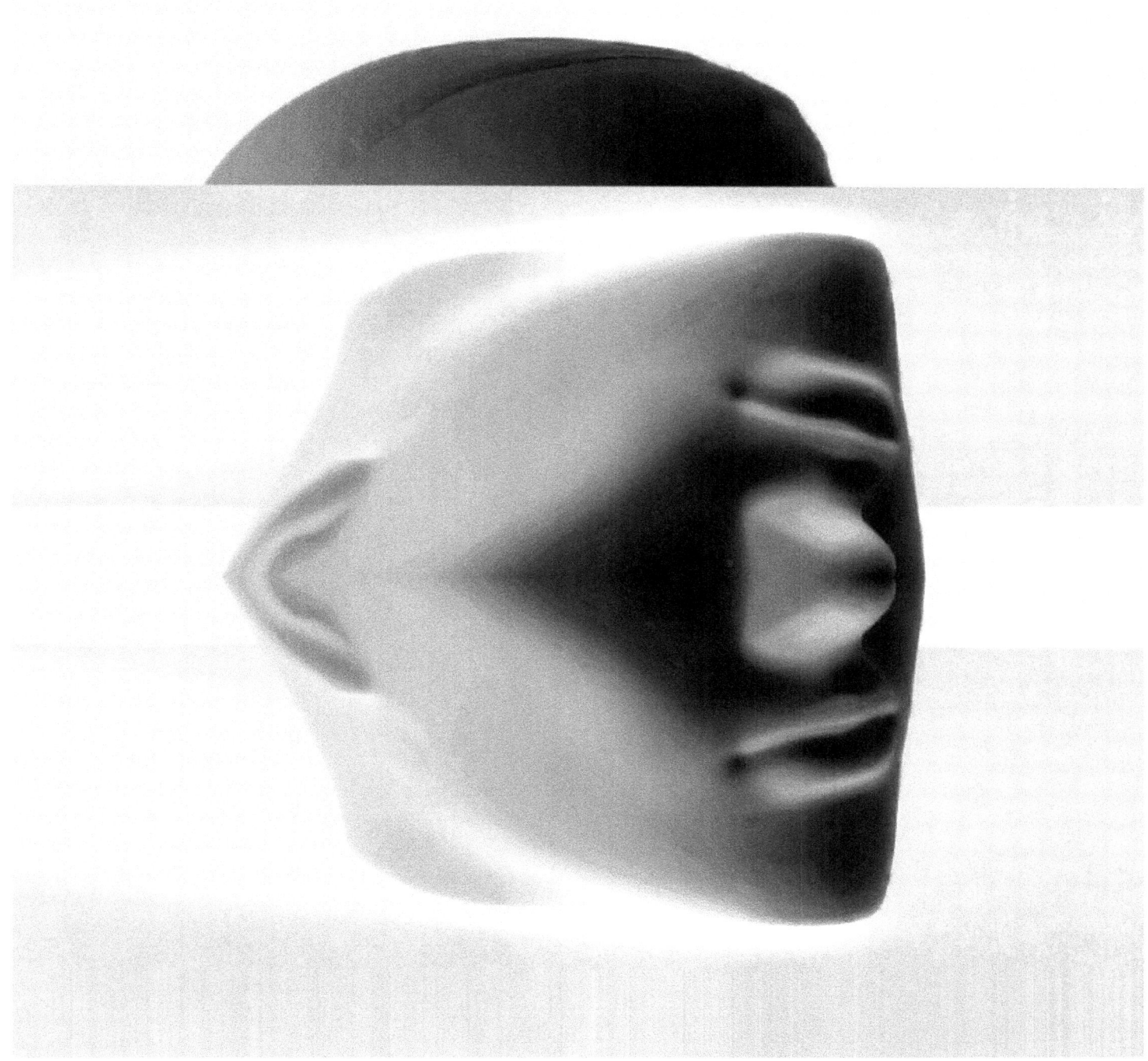

Suitable for a collage

Leah Ibrahim Sams (Founder & Artist of Power Of Women), *Arabella,* 1500x1500 px, PNG

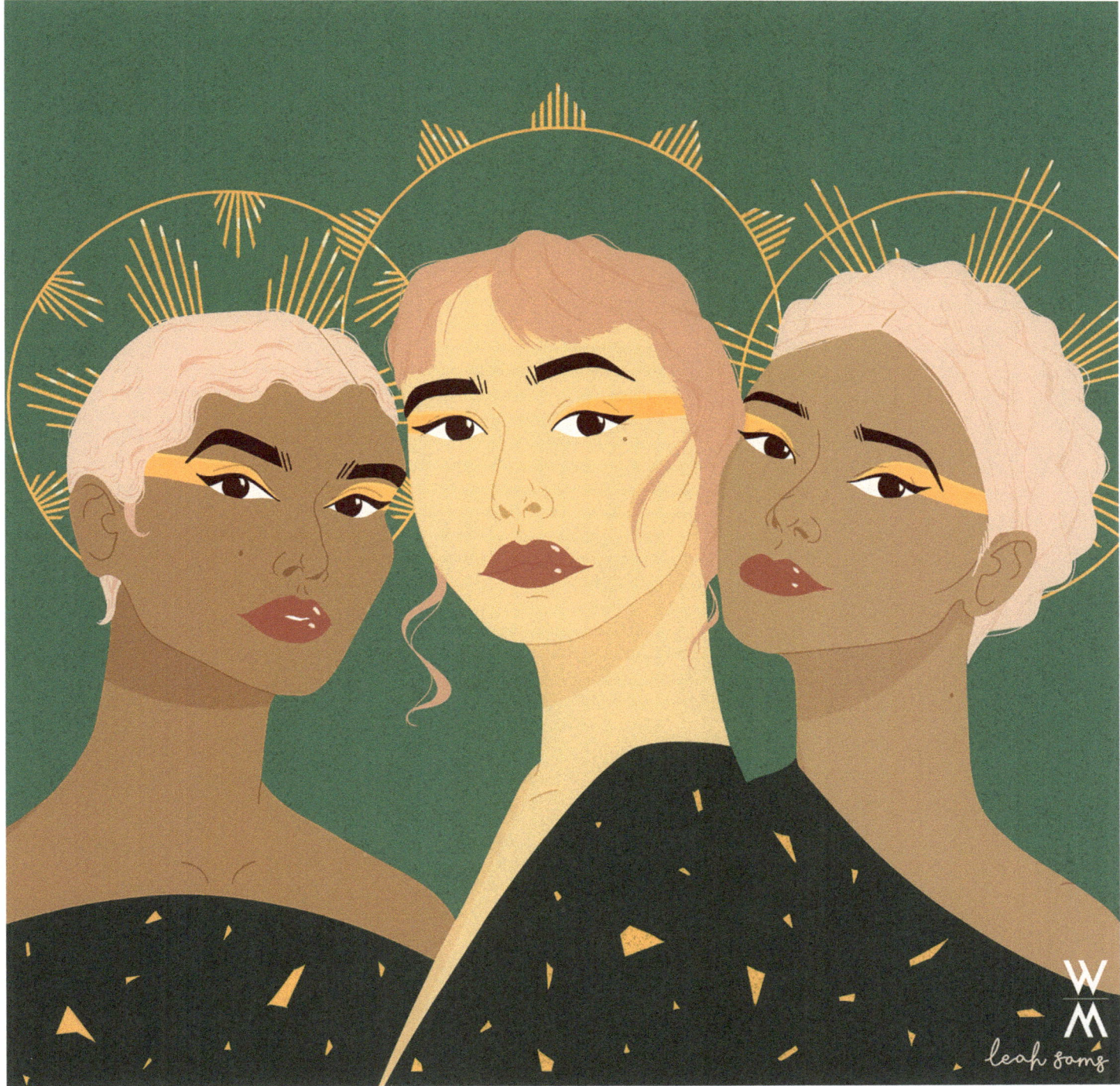